PERGAMON INTERNATIONAL LIBRARY
of Science, Technology, Engineering and Social Studies

*The 1000-volume original paperback library in aid of education,
industrial training and the enjoyment of leisure*

Publisher: Robert Maxwell, M.C.

LIV SJL

PEDIATRIC PSYCHOLOGY

Pergamon Titles of Related Interest

Cartledge/Milburn TEACHING SOCIAL SKILLS TO CHILDREN:
Innovative Approaches, Second edition
Johnson/Rasbury/Siegel APPROACHES TO CHILD TREATMENT:
Introduction to Theory, Research, and Practice
Morris/Blatt SPECIAL EDUCATION: Research and Trends
Plas SYSTEMS PSYCHOLOGY IN THE SCHOOLS
Santostefano COGNITIVE CONTROL THERAPY WITH
CHILDREN AND ADOLESCENTS
Wielkiewicz BEHAVIOR MANAGEMENT IN THE SCHOOLS:
Principles and Procedures

Related Journals
(Free sample copies available upon request)

CLINICAL PSYCHOLOGY REVIEW
JOURNAL OF CHILD PSYCHOLOGY AND PSYCHIATRY
JOURNAL OF SCHOOL PSYCHOLOGY

PSYCHOLOGY PRACTITIONER GUIDEBOOKS

EDITORS
Arnold P. Goldstein, Syracuse University
Leonard Krasner, SUNY at Stony Brook
Sol L. Garfield, Washington University

PEDIATRIC PSYCHOLOGY
Psychological Interventions and Strategies for Pediatric Problems

MICHAEL C. ROBERTS
The University of Alabama

PERGAMON PRESS
New York   Oxford   Beijing   Frankfurt   São Paulo   Sydney   Tokyo   Toronto

Pergamon Press Offices:

U.S.A.	Pergamon Press, Maxwell House, Fairview Park, Elmsford, New York 10523, U.S.A.
U.K.	Pergamon Press, Headington Hill Hall, Oxford OX3 0BW, England
PEOPLE'S REPUBLIC OF CHINA	Pergamon Press, Qianmen Hotel, Beijing, People's Republic of China
FEDERAL REPUBLIC OF GERMANY	Pergamon Press, Hammerweg 6, D-6242 Kronberg, Federal Republic of Germany
BRAZIL	Pergamon Editora, Rua Eça de Queiros, 346, CEP 04011, São Paulo, Brazil
AUSTRALIA	Pergamon Press (Aust.) Pty., P.O. Box 544, Potts Point, NSW 2011, Australia
JAPAN	Pergamon Press, 8th Floor, Matsuoka Central Building, 1-7-1 Nishishinjuku, Shinjuku-ku, Tokyo 160, Japan
CANADA	Pergamon Press Canada, Suite 104, 150 Consumers Road, Willowdale, Ontario M2J 1P9, Canada

First printing 1986

Library of Congress Cataloging in Publication Data

Roberts, Michael C.
    Pediatric psychology.

    (Psychology practitioner guidebooks)
    Bibliography: p.
    Includes index.
    1. Pediatrics--Psychological aspects. I. Title.
II. Series. [DNLM: 1. Child Psychology. 2 Mental
Disorders--in infancy and childhood. 3. Mental
Disorders--therapy. WS 105 R646p]
RJ47.5.R63 1986   618.92'89   86-5451
ISBN 0-08-032412-6
ISBN 0-08-032411-8 (pbk.)

Printed in the United States of America

This book is dedicated to the teachers of the Rolla, Missouri public school system

Contents

Preface   ix

Chapter

1. INTRODUCTION TO PEDIATRIC PSYCHOLOGY   1
    Rationale for Development of Pediatric Psychology   2
    Roles and Functions of Pediatric Psychologists   4
    Areas Related to Pediatric Psychology   5
    Overview of the Book   7

2. ORIENTATIONS OF PEDIATRIC PSYCHOLOGY PRACTICE   9
    Pediatric Psychology Practice   11
    Flexibility in Theoretical Approaches   12
    Preventing Mind Set   12
    Innovation and Creativity   15
    Pragmatic Orientation   17
    Developmental Perspective   18
    Types of Clinical Cases   19

3. CONSULTATION WITH PEDIATRICIANS
    AND ALLIED PERSONNEL   23
    Independent Functions Model   25
    Indirect Psychological Consultation Model   28
    Collaborative Team Model   32
    Pediatric Practice Consultation Orientation   35

4. PEDIATRIC PSYCHOLOGY PRACTICES   53
    Assessment   54
    Acute Physical Disorders   59
    Chronic Physical Disorders   64

Psychosomatic Disorders   68
Developmental Disorders   74
Psychological–Behavioral Problems   77
Prevention   80
Summary   86

5.   RESOURCES FOR PEDIATRIC PSYCHOLOGY   87
     Organizations and Journals   87
     Books and Articles   90

References   97

Author Index   111

Subject Index   118

About the Author   123

Psychology Practitioner Guidebooks List   125

Preface

In the course of my continuing development as a pediatric psychologist, I have had several excellent role models as teachers and supervisors. These include Donald Ottinger, Purdue University, and Logan Wright, University of Oklahoma, who sparked my interest in the field of pediatric psychology in my first semester of graduate work at Purdue. At the clinical internship at the University of Oklahoma Health Sciences Center were exceptional mentors — C. Eugene Walker, Diane Willis, and Arlene Schaefer. Since my formal education ended and the real learning started, professional and personal interactions with colleagues in the field have enhanced my knowledge of this field. Annette La Greca, Lizette Peterson, and Gerald Koocher have been particularly influential. The officers and members of the Society of Pediatric Psychology also have been special sources of valued professional stimulation.

Work with students in the clinical child psychology concentration at the University of Alabama, many of whom are now professionals in their own right, has helped to keep me active and knowledgeable, resulting from their growing understanding of the literature and clinical activities in pediatric psychology. Many of these people have been coauthors on articles and chapters with me and their indirect input to this book is immense: Sandy Wurtele, James Maddux, Pauline Elkins, James Schierberl, George Royal, Patricia Potter, Alcuin Johnson, Debra Fanurik, and David Layfield. I appreciate Polly Elkins' reading of an earlier draft of the manuscript.

I thank Yolandia Eubanks, my secretary, for her tolerance during the writing and editing. She smilingly cleaned up my cluttered diskettes to produce a readable manuscript. My wife, Karen, and children, Erica and Alicia, also deserve my thanks and love for putting up with this book and me.

This book is dedicated to my primary and secondary education school teachers in Rolla, Missouri, starting with Mrs. Christopher's kindergarten and extending through Mrs. Jensen's senior English, with memorable and treasured teachers in between. Teachers are often underappreciated or only valued long after one leaves the classroom. It is too late for me to extend thanks to some of my teachers. Of course, although this book is dedicated to those who labored to educate me, the errors are mine, not theirs.

Michael C. Roberts
Tuscaloosa, Alabama
January, 1986

Chapter 1

Introduction to Pediatric Psychology

Case 1: Oscar was a 5-month-old infant at a children's hospital emergency room presenting with symptoms of diarrhea, gastroenteritis, and upper respiratory infection. Oscar's weight, height, and head circumferences were below the 3rd percentile on a growth chart for his age. The pediatrician diagnosed his condition as "failure to thrive secondary to maternal deprivation syndrome." (Roberts & Horner, 1979)

Case 2: Karen was a 10-year-old who complained to her parents and pediatrician of severe stomach pains for over a year. She frequently missed school. The pain was nonspecifically described as a dull ache in the epigastric and umbilical regions, with durations lasting from a few minutes up to an hour. However, no organic cause for the pains could be determined. (Miller & Kratochwill, 1979)

Case 3: Joey, a 4-year-old boy, was retaining feces for periods of a few days to a week at a time. He was soiling his underpants and occasionally passing whole bowel movements into his clothing, even though he had been toilet trained for 2 years. This condition was of 18-months duration. Bowel abnormalities were ruled out as contributing to the fecal retention. (Roberts, Ottinger, & Hannemann, 1977)

Case 4: Amy, a 9-year-old girl with juvenile diabetes, had been repeatedly hospitalized with medical complications because of her failure to follow the diabetic treatment regimen. Despite detailed instruction on diet, urine testing, and insulin injections, Amy was noncompliant with the medical regimen. (Lowe & Lutzker, 1979)

Case 5: Annette was a 6-year-old girl with a diagnosis of acute lymphatic leukemia. In 7 months, she had experienced seven bone marrow aspirations. During these painful procedures, she became highly anxious and uncooperative, cried loudly, and complained of pain. (Hilgard & LeBaron, 1982)

Case 6: Another Amy, an 8-year-old girl, was burned over 80% of her body in a gas heater fire. At first, she was delirious and survival was precarious.

> Later she became fearful of medical procedures, actively resisted treat-
> ment, refused to eat, and resisted practicing physiotherapy exercises.
> (Walker & Healy, 1980)

These types of clinical cases frequently occur in pediatric settings such as pediatricians' offices, clinics, and children's hospitals. They are rarely seen in traditional psychiatric or clinical child psychology practices. Yet, these cases and many
more illustrate the range of problems daily confronting pediatricians and psychologists in medical settings. Pediatric psychology developed as a professional specialty within the mental health profession because of such many different clinical
problems and skills required to intervene successfully. This book will discuss the
variety of these presenting problems and their psychological interventions.

The specialty of pediatric psychology combines aspects of several approaches
in the delivery of health care to children and their families. This field came into
existence primarily to fill an unmet need: Pediatric physicians are confronted with
a large number of problems that require a comprehensive medical–psychological
treatment approach much like the ones presented in the opening of this chapter.
Indeed, in a study of pediatric practices, only 12% of all patients presented problems that were considered purely physical; 36% had problems that were considered to be psychological, and the remaining 52% had problems that were both
physical and psychological in nature (Duff, Rowe, & Anderson, 1973).

As a result of such demands in their actual practice, pediatricians recognized
the emotional and psychological aspects of the problems they treat everyday. At
the same time, psychologists discovered the varied types of psychopathology
related to organic illnesses and, more importantly, the utility of behavioral interventions for some medical disorders.

A "new marriage" of psychology and pediatrics was proposed several years ago
(Kagan, 1965), with a general strengthening of ties between the professions as
time has passed (Wright, 1985). The marriage has not been without problems
and, in some situations, pediatricians and psychologists remain together through
coexistence (not collaboration) for the "sake of the children." In many ways, however, the relationships of pediatricians and psychologists have been mutually beneficial for the professionals and greatly advantageous for many patients and their
families. Although this book is not a "marriage" handbook, it is hoped that a
discussion of the consultative relationships between pediatricians and psychologists and of their conjoint activities will be productive in promoting this union of
disciplines and individual professionals.

RATIONALE FOR DEVELOPMENT
OF PEDIATRIC PSYCHOLOGY

The specialty of pediatric psychology developed as pediatric and psychological
practitioners found they could not meet the challenge of critical childhood problems from within the frameworks of either traditional pediatrics or traditional

clinical child psychology. As noted in the Duff et al. study (1973) and others, the types of problems presenting in pediatric practices involve a significant number of psychological, developmental, behavioral, educational, and child-management issues. According to one study, 37% of all "well-child" visits to pediatricians involved support and counseling for issues of child rearing and behavioral management (McClelland, Staples, Weisberg, & Berger, 1973). An additional 19% of parents' questions to pediatricians concerned academic performance. Thus, over half of the questions asked of pediatricians during routine office visits are concerned with nonmedical topics. Unfortunately, the practicing pediatrician usually has had inadequate training to competently manage these types of problems, likely has little personal proclivity to treat them, and may need more time to focus on medical problems (Roberts & Wright, 1982).

Mental health services for children and their families have also been inadequate. According to the Children's Defense Fund, two thirds of the three million seriously emotionally disturbed children in the United States are not getting mental health services (Knitzer, 1982). Furthermore, when children are seen in traditional mental health settings such as outpatient psychiatric clinics, child guidance clinics, or psychological service centers, children and their parents have often gone through a shaping process because they have been interviewed, diagnosed, and referred on to another agency (Walker, 1979a). This shaping sometimes changes the patient's behavior, responses to questions, motivation, and perceptions of helping professionals.

Consequently, pediatric psychology developed as a result of these two phenomena: Pediatricians require psychological services to meet the needs of their practices, and psychologists have the goal to provide more accessible, competent services for children and families needing psychological interventions. A productive collaboration thus resulted in the specialty of pediatric psychology. The specialty did not spring forth overnight, but emerged over time as individual professionals sought each other's assistance.

Pediatric psychology has developed a unique constellation of characteristics. As will be seen in this book, these include such aspects as : (a) clinical practice, often in a health care setting; (b) a medically based referral mechanism and source of clients; (c) an orientation to health promotion and problem prevention to enhance children's development or to return children to normal developmental pathways; (d) an emphasis on developmental considerations; (e) consultation to physicians and parents, with some direct intervention with child patients; and (f) a practical orientation to treatment techniques that are demonstrably effective, time-efficient, and economical.

Because pediatric psychologists often practice in a health-care setting rather than a psychiatric one, they encounter patient problems that can vary widely from those encountered by a traditional clinical child psychologist. Although some types of problems are seen in all settings (e.g., children noncompliant with parents, children with academic difficulties), other disorders frequently seen in pediatric psychology settings are relatively rare in other settings.

Pediatric psychological problems that are commonly presented include psychological–behavioral concomitants of physical illness, handicap, or medical procedures (e.g., sequelae to burns, spina bifida, or meningitis, adjustment to diabetes or hemophilia, anxiety over surgical hospitalization or bone marrow aspiration). Additionally, there is a wide range of medical–psychological disorders for which effective psychological interventions are available (e.g., encopresis, failure to thrive, abdominal pain).

Similarly, psychological interventions are showing value in changing child and parent behaviors to healthier ones and to ones that prevent injuries (e.g., teaching nutritional habits, motivating seat belt use). The orientation towards improvement of children's health frequently takes the pediatric psychologist out of the medical setting and into schools, day care centers, playgrounds, homes, shopping malls— in short, wherever children are and where interventions for health improvement might be effective.

ROLES AND FUNCTIONS OF PEDIATRIC PSYCHOLOGISTS

The pediatric psychologist typically, but not always, works in a medical or a primary health-care setting. These may include hospitals, clinics, pediatric practices, developmental centers, and health maintenance organizations, although many interventions may take place outside of these settings. The medical setting is basically nonpsychiatric, that is, the primary focus is not mental health, but physical health.

There are several implications from this medical setting aspect. First, the pediatric psychologist is usually at the point of the patient's initial presentation for help, because the majority of problems are first presented in medical settings. In contrast, the typical psychiatric or mental health center is both physically and conceptually away from the site of a problem's initial presentation and may require a cumbersome referral procedure to get the patient and family to appropriate services. Second, as a consequence of the pediatric psychological practice setting, the presenting problems are seen in their earlier stages of development, usually before they have become moderately or severely debilitating. Early intervention in these pediatric settings often precludes the process of "shaping" the patient or parent to give standardized responses through a series of referrals (Walker, 1979a). Third, as noted before, the problems include a higher number of medically related disorders, although problems of a strictly behavioral nature are sometimes present. Fourth, the diagnostic workups and the therapeutic interventions are typically briefer and more specifically targeted.

A number of writers have outlined various types of schemes to conceptualize the role of the pediatric psychologist—including consultant, information resource, educator, facilitator, counselor, conferring diagnostician, therapist, researcher, and innovator. Frequently, in practice the pediatric psychologist may serve in multiple roles, often at the same time. I have found that pediatric psychologists do not wear one "hat," but may wear several different hats, depending upon the situation. Rather than envision the psychologist putting on and taking off various hats, I visualize pediatric psychologists wearing one hat with several bills that are quickly turned forward as the case requires a shift in roles. Later chapters elaborate upon these various roles. Much of the excitement and challenge of pediatric psychology derives from the multitude of roles and functions the professional can assume.

AREAS RELATED TO PEDIATRIC PSYCHOLOGY

There are several terms used to designate many of the interests and activities I categorize as "pediatric psychology." Unfortunately, sometimes too much fuss can be made over terminology and labels. Many terms have arisen to describe various components of psychology applied to medical and health matters, some specific to children or pediatrics. Some authors claim that precision in terminology aids communication. Indeed, at times the terms proposed convey a specific connotation or emphasis. All too often, though, these terms may add to the confusion of what the specialty is and what professionals are doing. In this section, I am juxtaposing the various terms and their definitions, not strictly as an academic exercise, but in order to clarify the role and scope of pediatric psychology.

Proceeding from more general terms to the more specific, various practitioners and writers have referred to the involvement of psychologists in medical and health matters such as medical psychology, behavioral medicine, health psychology, behavioral health, behavioral pediatrics, developmental and behavioral pediatrics, pediatric psychology, and a few others. These terms have been defined as follows:

Medical psychology: "The study of psychological factors related to all aspects of physical health, illness, and its treatment at the individual, group, and systems level" (Asken, 1975, p. 67).

Behavioral medicine: "Behavioral medicine is the interdisciplinary field concerned with the development and integration of behavioral and biomedical science knowledge and techniques relevant to health and illness and the application of this knowledge and these techniques to prevention, diagnosis, treatment and rehabilitation" (Schwartz & Weiss, 1978, p. 7).

Health psychology: "Health psychology is the aggregate of the specific educational, scientific, and professional contributions of the discipline of psychology to the promotion and maintenance of health, the prevention and treatment of illness, and the identification of etiologic and diagnostic correlates of health, illness, and related dysfunctions, and to the analysis and improvement of the health care system and health policy formation" (Division of Health Psychology, undated, p. 1).

Behavioral health: "Behavioral health is an interdisciplinary field dedicated to promoting a philosophy of health that stresses individual responsibility in the application of behavioral and biomedical science knowledge and techniques to the maintenance of health and the prevention of illness and dysfunction by a variety of self-initiated individual or shared activities" (Matarazzo, 1980, p. 813).

Behavioral pediatrics: "Behavioral pediatrics represents the interdisciplinary integration between biobehavioral science and pediatric medicine, with an emphasis on multidimensional and comprehensive diagnosis, prevention, treatment, and rehabilitation of physical disease and disabilities in children and adolescents" (Varni & Dietrich, 1981, p. 5). "Behavioral pediatrics focuses particularly on issues such as psychological factors contributing to the etiology of various childhood diseases (e.g., asthma), the psychological sequelae of various medical problems (e.g., cardiac surgery, leukemia), and psychological factors that contribute to the maintenance of adequate medical care (e.g., compliance in children with juvenile diabetes)" (La Greca & Stone, 1985, p. 255).

Developmental and behavioral pediatrics: "Developmental pediatrics has concerned itself largely with cognitive competence and the associated physical and mental disabilities that constrain function in childhood. Behavioral pediatrics has emphasized the prevention and treatment of disorders of personality and the effects of family function and social adaptation. *Developmental-behavioral pediatrics* splices these strands together so as to emphasize their shared themes, their compatible missions, and their complementary contributions to general pediatrics and other disciplines concerned with health and function in childhood" (Levine, Carey, Crocker, & Gross, 1983, p. xv).

Pediatric Psychology: "Pediatric psychology as a field of research and practice has been concerned with a wide variety of topics in the relationship between the psychological and physical well-being of children, including behavioral and emotional concomitants of disease and illness, the role of psychology in pediatric medicine, and the promotion of health and prevention of illness among healthy children" (Roberts, Maddux, & Wright, 1984, pp. 56-57).

Many other terms have surfaced to cover the field or certain aspects within it: child health psychology (Karoly, Steffen, & O'Grady, 1982), clinical behavioral pediatrics (Varni, 1983), biosocial pediatrics (Green, 1980), pediatric behavioral medicine (Williams, Foreyt, & Goodrick, 1981), and child health care psychology (Wright, 1979b).

As can be seen, there has been a proliferation of terms describing the area of psychological applications to medical- or health-related phenomena. All of these terms seem to describe about the same thing despite the advocates' assertions that new and improved concepts are being advanced. The final definition of pediatric psychology appears to be not much different from the various terms just presented.

Why bother with this seemingly academic exercise of definitions? *First,* I think the terms have been confusing and too often used in such a restricting way as to impede development of the field. This is the case of "behavioral medicine," where many professionals thought "behavioral" referred to behavioral therapy, when it actually reflected more general behavioral sciences (Masur, 1979). This confusion was perpetuated by the origins of the Society of Behavioral Medicine in the Association for the Advancement of Behavior Therapy. Similarly, debates over health psychology and health-care psychology seem overdrawn. *Second*, these terms and their definitions coalesce to form a verbal image of this field that encompasses psychological research and applications to medical and health phenomena.

In this book, the emphasis within this large domain will be children, youth, and families. The term *pediatric psychology* is used to cover the generic field of practice and research of psychological applications to pediatric problems and children's health (Wright, 1967). Examples of applications and research are drawn from a variety of sources that sometimes have a narrower, more specific orientation to one or another term. In the final analysis, however, I have found pediatric psychology is broad enough to cover all of the various activities and interests.

The actual activities of pediatric psychologists with their varied types of cases and research define the field much better than the specific terminology or its formal definitions can. The six cases in this chapter's opening present just a few examples of the wide range of clinical problems confronting the practitioner. These cases will be followed up later in this book to illustrate assessment and intervention techniques. Additionally, many more clinical problems will be discussed. In the *Encyclopedia of Pediatric Psychology,* Wright, Schaefer, and Solomons (1979) examine 114 entities and their concomitants. Since their desk reference was published, many more problems have arisen for which pediatric psychology has shown its usefulness in facilitating understanding and successful intervention.

OVERVIEW OF THE BOOK

This book will provide a basic introduction and orientation to the field of pediatric psychology through a pragmatic approach to case conceptualization and consultation. Pediatric psychology possesses a unique constellation of characteristics, including: (a) referral and practice in the health-care setting, (b) emphasis on developmental processes, (c) consultation and collaboration with medical personnel, and (d) psychological interventions for behavioral concomitants of physical disorders and for medical-physical disorders for which psychology offers effective treatment.

In chapter 2, the orientations of pediatric psychologists will be considered as a background for the types of practice and cases seen by the practitioner. In chapter 3, the role of the pediatric psychologist as consultant will be examined as an important aspect of practice. Important practical issues of consultation–liaison will be detailed. Chapter 4 will consider the areas of pediatric psychology practice, including developmental assessment, acute and chronic physical disorders, psychosomatic disorders, developmental disorders, psychological–behavioral problems, and prevention. Finally, chapter 5 will annotate useful resources for the pediatric psychologist. The book is intended to draw together information from research and clinical practice to provide the pediatric psychology practitioner with a broad sense of this exciting field.

Chapter 2
Orientations of Pediatric Psychology Practice

The current nature of pediatric practice itself influences the orientation and practice of pediatric psychologists more than any other aspect. Much of the pediatrician's time in outpatient practice is spent on well-child checkups (about 50%), with an additional 20% devoted to minor medical problems (Bergman, Dassel, & Wedgewood, 1966). The pattern of problems presenting in office-based pediatric practices appears to be shifting from disease-oriented visits to contacts concerning academic performance and learning disabilities (up 60%) and child behavioral management (up 40%) (Burnett & Bell, 1978). There have been important changes in children's mortality and morbidity patterns. This shift is most likely caused by improved medical procedures, including prevention through immunization, nutrition, and early detection of developing problems, with corresponding changes in pediatric practice (Rogers, Blendon, & Hearn, 1981). Studies of pediatric offices revealed that the pediatrician spends an average of 13 minutes for each child patient, seeing an average of 27 outpatients per day (Bergman et al., 1966; Burnett, Williams, & Olmsted, 1978).

Thus far, pediatric office practice has been discussed, because this is where the majority of pediatric patients are seen. In contrast, the nature of practice in hospital-based pediatrics and related medical specialties remains oriented to services for chronic illness and acute, severe medical problems.

Medical evaluation and treatment are also constrained by time in the hospital inpatient practice of pediatrics. Pediatricians and hospital-attending physicians must diagnose and start treatment of many patients per day, focusing on the physical–medical problems of most active concern at the time. Thus, the inpatient and outpatient pediatric practices are quite similar in demands on time and energy, with corresponding limitations on attention to psychosocial aspects.

Most pediatricians are clinically oriented, with a strong emphasis on the physical component of a patient. This focus results from their training, which emphasizes biochemical, viral, and bacteriological aspects of medical problems. Indeed, much of pediatric training is taken in large medical centers where the major focus is on inpatient work with children who have life-threatening or handicapping diseases and conditions, because such centers are typically tertiary-care facilities. In practice, however, hospitalization for acute illnesses has declined 65% (Burnett & Bell, 1978). Similarly, as noted earlier, relatively little of an office practice or primary care pediatrician's time is spent on purely physical problems; more time is spent on well-child, anticipatory guidance, and child management issues. Nonetheless, pediatricians and other medical professionals are often more comfortable with and interested in medical–physical aspects of patients than with their psychological–behavioral issues. This focus was made clear one time when I lectured to medical students on the psychological phenomena of children and diabetes. I spoke on adjustment issues, patients' understanding of the disease, enhancing medical regimen compliance, and developmental considerations of self-care and adjustment, only to have the first question asked of me (a psychologist): "What's the process by which insulin osmoses through the cell wall?" Needless to say, I was irritated, but not greatly surprised that their attention was not directed to what *I* thought were the most important aspects of diabetes care.

Similarly, Bernstein, Sanger, and Fras (1969) describe hospital medical personnel's tendency to disregard psychological considerations of treatment while attending solely to medical issues. On a children's burn unit, Bernstein et al. indicated that medical staff debated "epithelialization of a skin graft or dehydration . . . rather than the problems of depression and separation, which produced refusal to eat and drink, thus causing dehydration and failure of grafts" (p. 636).

Medical schools often select students based largely on performance in science and mathematics courses, so it follows that these students as later practitioners maintain their interests in such phenomena. These responses and behaviors can be puzzling and frustrating to the psychologist. They often cause one to wonder if whether attempting to consult is worth the effort. The temptation is also great to berate physicians for their ignorance or arrogance over psychosocial issues. One must resist this temptation, because it is not totally accurate and certainly such an attitude on the part of psychologists is nonproductive. The psychologist may have to turn his or her hat with many bills to show the *educator* side of the bill and diplomatically expand our allied professionals' range of knowledge and information. Chapter 3 will describe models of pediatric consultation that often permit educative roles for the psychologist.

All of this should not suggest that pediatricians have no interest in psychosocial issues of their practice. Indeed, many observers believe pediatricians are more aware of and attentive to these issues than are other medical specialists. In the 1970s there was a renewed emphasis in medical education on training these "primary health care physicians" to recognize and treat psychosocial problems in their practices (Wright, 1978b). Medical school curricula and continuing education programs increasingly included prenatal health and psychosomatic issues. By necessity, however, the amount of time and effort in education that can be given to these topics is a great deal less than that given to the physical aspects of pediatrics. The initiative to improve psychological roles of primary health care physicians now seems to be attenuated. The integration of the psychological aspects of pediatrics remains seriously neglected except where individual pediatricians take on the task themselves of learning and applying them to their own practices. A relatively small number of pediatricians have now devoted their practices to developmental-behavioral pediatrics, although the vast majority continue the more traditional approaches.

The nature of pediatric/medical training is an important determinant of how the psychologist is viewed and consulted with, as well as how the psychologist adjusts to and works in this type of setting and attitude. The general attention to physical components to the neglect of psychological ones presents a hindrance in some ways and a challenge in other ways. If pediatricians had the interest, time, and training to provide adequate psychosocial services, there might be little need for pediatric psychologists.

PEDIATRIC PSYCHOLOGY PRACTICE

More pediatric psychologists currently practice in hospital or medical institutional settings, even though more pediatric patients are seen in outpatient settings. Roles for psychologists in outpatient pediatric clinics are increasing, however, and future trends may open up more roles for psychologists in outpatient clinics and practices.

The nature of pediatric practice in offices and hospitals influences the nature of pediatric psychological practices in these settings. In any setting, there are several implications for the psychologist consulting or providing services. First, the pediatrician has very little free time and must push to keep up with the demands of practice. Second, the brevity of pediatrician–patient contact likely reflects the larger number of well-child visits in office practice. A third implication is that psychological consultation to the pediatrician needs to be similarly brief and to the point. Finally, psychological interventions often need to be briefly implemented and fairly short-term in most cases. These last two implications require the psychologist to relinquish some cherished notions about traditional clinical child psychological practice, especially those regarding extensive diagnostic workups and lengthy treatments. As a result of these implications, the pediatric psychologist uses techniques that are more economical and demonstrably effective. Behavioral techniques and crisis intervention are the most frequently used strategies.

When the pediatric psychologist works collaboratively with the pediatrician, or any medical specialist, the consultation should be brief and targeted to the most important considerations. For example, in hospital-based consultation, Hartlage and Hartlage (1978) recommend short psychological "curbside consultations," in the hallway if necessary, to remedy the problem of inadequate time. This type of consultation appears hasty and informal, but it can provide valuable information and establish a consultation conducive to pediatric practice.

Additionally, targeted, to-the-point psychological reports are more likely to be read and utilized by the pediatrician than are lengthy, esoteric reports containing great quantities of psychological jargon. Walker (1979a) suggests tightly worded, action-based reports communicating what should be done about a patient's problem. Typical reports from pediatric psychologists do not ramble on and on about background information; they do not elaborate test data and personality descriptions. These reports by necessity usually indicate the problem and referral question, give a brief exposition of what was done and what was found, and place the greatest emphasis on what is recommended to be done. Lee Salk (1985), reminiscing about early days of pediatric psychology, reported an occurrence that has happened to many detailed evaluations, when only the first and last pages of reports were retained and actually read by the referring pediatricians. Thus, understanding the brevity of patient contact in pediatric work influences the psychologist's consultation regardless of a hospital or office practice setting.

FLEXIBILITY IN THEORETICAL APPROACHES

The culture and nature of pediatric practice strongly influences the psychological practice in pediatric settings. The selection of assessment and treatment intervention similarly is affected by the types of presenting problems and the quick-paced nature of medically related work. In response to practice demands for efficient and effective interventions, behavioral strategies frequently are implemented, although by no means is pediatric psychology solely in the behavioral camp. Practitioners have found, however, that in many cases behavioral interventions can be more demonstrably effective, briefer, more targeted to specific clinical problems, and easier to implement by pediatricians and allied personnel as well as parents (Roberts, Maddux, Wurtele, & Wright, 1982; Walker, 1979a, 1979b) than are more traditional psychiatric or psychological therapies.

Yet, pediatric psychological practice may be classified more as multitheoretical or "theoretically ambidextrous" because many practitioners and researchers function within many various theoretical orientations. The flexibility of such eclecticism allows the practitioner to respond more appropriately to individual patients with particular problems and situations. Most practitioners have resisted rigidity and becoming too set in one theoretical camp or another.

PREVENTING MIND SET

The pediatric psychologist frequently sees clinical cases that differ in such important ways as to preclude the rigid application of techniques successfully used on somewhat similar cases. Thus, pediatric psychologists find it important to avoid the problem of "mind set" in approaching each case. Mind set implies that all similar cases (e.g., of enuresis or failure to thrive) can be treated with the same treatment protocols (e.g., toilet training by the techniques of Azrin & Foxx, 1974). Mind set even goes so far as to say that *all* cases can be treated by one type of intervention (e.g., "everything is remediable through operant conditioning" or "all child patients will gain from play therapy"). Although easy to disparage in the abstract, there is a real tendency to categorize problems and approach them in consistent ways. This tendency is illustrated in the contrasting of two cases.

At the beginning of chapter 1, Case 2 described Karen as a 10-year-old having frequent stomachaches with no organic causes. She missed school because of her pain complaints. Karen reported stomachaches on the average of one and a half per day. Her school performance was average, and she had no other social–behavioral problems. Karen's mother attended to these complaints by providing her with TV, snacks, toys, and social interaction. The consulting psychologists conceptualized the pain reports as being maintained by reinforcement. Consequently, the treatment involved time-out procedures where, upon complaining of pain, Karen was put in her room for a rest, with the curtains closed and light on. She could read books but not watch TV or play games. Meals were provided as scheduled with no extra snacks. The time-out procedure remained in place from the point of complaint to the end of the day. This behavioral intervention reduced the frequency of stomach pains with a 1-year follow-up indicating no further reports (Miller & Kratochwill, 1979).

A case very similar to Karen's is that of Stephen, a 14-year-old boy who had an 18-month history of reporting abdominal pains with diarrhea and nausea (Stabler, 1979). These problems led to three hospitalizations, once for exploratory surgery, and considerable absences from school. Extensive medical evaluations determined no physical cause for the pain complaints. The tendency might be for the consulting psychologist to approach Stephen as he or she did Karen. Thus, an operant-based intervention would be devised, with restrictions on Stephen whenever he complained of stomach pains and rewards when he refrained from complaints. However, this approach would be mind set. Such a rigid, blind application would probably have failed to help Stephen, even though the operant treatment helped resolve Karen's problems. In Stephen's case, upon further information gathering, the consulting psychologist and social workers found that his father had died of stomach cancer 2 years previously. Stephen appeared to be out of touch with his emotions, relying on repression and denial as defense mechanisms. The treatment intervention involved providing psychological support and aiding return to school through collaboration with the school counselor (Stabler, 1979). An operant-based program might have changed Stephen's pain complaints, but not have helped his adjustment to his father's death.

In order to avoid mind set, pediatric psychologists tend to accept and function well with a number of theoretical orientations and treatment modalities. Of course, one might argue that any good psychologist would investigate other aspects of a patient's situation before instituting treatment. Yet, we must recognize that this is all too often not the case. Medical lore holds that physicians are like workers who see horses day in and day out — horses in such a variety of colors and shapes that when they do see a zebra, they may not recognize it as a species separate from horses. Because pediatricians and pediatric psychologists see many children with somatic complaints, it is important to recognize the variety of precipitating and perpetuating factors that may lead to different treatment approaches. Similarly, psychologists and other professionals see a multitude of noncompliant children, for example, and when a variation presents, they may not recognize the changed situation or behavior and may treat it as just another noncompliance case. The mind set problem is one with which many professionals can become afflicted, and one that *all* must attempt to avoid.

Theoretical versatility in pediatric psychology also is required because many of the problems facing the practitioner have not been remedied previously. When a novel case presents itself, as often happens in pediatric psychology, there may be no existing research or literature on the particular problem to assist the practitioner in formulating a case conceptualization and intervention. Additionally, where presenting cases are similar to published studies, the literature usually contains insufficient detail or information with which to apply the intervention procedures to the new case. In pediatric psychology, as in much of professional psychology, there is a need to individualize, adapt, create, and innovate.

As a case in point, Logan Wright (1971), one of the founding pediatric psychologists, described how he developed a treatment methodology for children's refusals to swallow liquids or solids. At the time he received the referrals, there was very little literature on increasing children's consumption responses, even though the condition had been well recognized previously and could prove life-threatening. Wright was confronted with three girls, two who refused fluids and another who refused solids and fluids. While attempting to use a toy and social reinforcement to induce fluid acceptance with the first patient, a 3-year, 9-month-old girl with Down's syndrome, Wright noticed that the girl laughed when she took a felt-tipped fountain pen from his pocket, pulled it apart, and dropped both pieces to the floor. Applying the Premack Principle, Wright then extended his observations and used this pen "toy" in an operant conditioning program to reinforce the girl's consuming fluids with successful results. This story illustrates how serendipity, careful observation, and reasoning play major roles in pediatric psychology endeavors wherein the practitioner continually faces new situations requiring innovation or modification of standardized techniques.

Similar instances illustrate that mind set has no place in pediatric psychology practice. A behaviorally trained psychologist may find considerable applications in pediatric oncology, for example. A useful behavioral technique might include making access to video games contingent upon reduced anticipatory distress associated with chemotherapy (Kolko & Rickard-Figueroa, 1985). However, it is also likely that nonbehavioral interventions of psychotherapy and supportive counseling are necessary for a patient's and family's adjustment, through expressions of fears, anger, frustrations, and the myriad of other emotions during cancer diagnosis and treatment (Koocher & Sallan, 1978; Spinetta et al., 1982). Thus, in just one pediatric division, hematology–oncology, the psychologist might need to be fluent in a variety of theoretical modalities for satisfactory treatment of the various psychological needs. Mind set or rigid applications of set protocols would be nonresponsive to the patients' problems.

INNOVATION AND CREATIVITY

Innovation and creativity are frequently required in the treatment of the constantly changing set of clinical problems in pediatric psychology. Mind set or theoretical rigidity, instead of innovative and creative applications, would interfere with successful remediation of these problems. To illustrate this point, I turn to one of the most common problems facing parents, pediatricians, and psychologists for decades: toilet training. Large sets of literature for professionals and for parents have developed to teach how to assess when to begin training, how to do it, and how to cope with special problems during it. Some of these procedures (e.g., Azrin & Foxx, 1974) have been empirically evaluated, others have not. Most of the attention in publications is given to urine training, that is, getting the child to use the toilet for urination. Indeed, many training procedures rely on rewards for appropriate urination with the number of urine training trials increased by having the child drink fluids that have diuretic action (e.g., Kool-Aid).

What is often missing in this literature is attention to training bowel habits. It is often assumed that somehow once urine retention and evacuation are trained, then the bowel movements will follow. Sometimes mention is made that while the child is sitting on the toilet, defecation may occur, and this is to be rewarded. Problems with bowel habit training are rarely mentioned except for the disorder of encopresis (soiling due to feces retention and impaction). When these problems of defecation occur, there is little preexisting literature on which to base intervention.

In my own practice, I have had referrals for children who had been urine trained for some time, but were not potty trained for their bowel movements. These older children, a girl and a boy in different families (ages 4 and 6 years, respectively), had continued to use diapers for defecating long past their need for urination. Although in regular underpants all day long, when they felt the urge to defecate, they simply asked for a diaper. A refusal by the parent would be met with tears and eventual withholding of the stool until the diaper was provided. These children were not encopretic and had been referred by pediatricians who had ruled out physical abnormalities (e.g., Hirschsprung's disease) as the cause. I could find no mention in existing literature on treatments for this problem. Several theoretical ideas came to mind: fixation in the anal stage, negative assertion of autonomy, conditioned fear of the toilet, among others. I could find no evidence of general behavioral noncompliance in these children, and they evidenced no fear of the toilet or bathroom, because they urinated there. Bowel movements were not painful or anxiety provoking; they were simply made into a diaper, not the commode.

I finally conceptualized the problem as being one of an unfortunate learning history, wherein the children learned proper urination habits due to the greater frequency of training trials, but they did not learn the proper defecation habits either due to low frequency or to situational learning of other responses. The boy defecated into his diapers while laying on his stomach, whereas the girl defecated in a slightly crouching position. Accordingly, I arranged for the parents to reward the children contingent upon gradually changing their posture while defecating into diapers. A hierarchy of postural changes was set up for each child to change position and more closely approximate sitting down. The last two positions were defecating into a loosened diaper while sitting on the toilet and finally into the toilet itself.

The treatment approach is readily identifiable as behavioral and involving shaping or successive approximations, perhaps with some systematic desensitization for fears of the commode and rewards for successful toilet use. I also speculate that these children may have learned to use certain muscles in defecation while in a certain position over the years and could not use the necessary (and more commonly used) muscles in order to defecate in the more traditional and conventional sitting position.

These two cases are similar to another case of a boy who had Hirschsprung's disease—a neurological condition of absence of nerve endings in the colon that, consequently, do not signal when the bowel is full and needs to be moved. This condition requires surgery to correct, but is symptomatically similar in some ways to encopresis or psychogenic constipation. The corrective surgery is typically done in infancy when the disease is usually first diagnosed. However, this boy's problems were not detected until age 2 1/2 years when the rather painful surgical repair took place. He had been urine trained but not trained for bowel movements. This appeared to be due to the Hirschsprung's disease and to the problematic way he had been medically treated before surgery with painful suppositories and harassment over resistance to the toilet. This continued for several months after the surgery when most children with this condition assume normal bowel functioning. He would wear a diaper at night and pass bowel movements in his sleep.

I first conceptualized the problem as being one of fear of the toilet and the pain previously experienced. I embarked upon a relaxation regimen using audiocassette tapes with visual imagery and tense-relax exercises (Koeppen, 1974). I also incorporated play therapy sessions that dealt with his reactions to the medical treatments and surgery. This approach had no success in increasing appropriate defecation, although it seemed to aid in the child's posthospitalization adjustment. Shifting conceptual gears, I then set up a systematic desensitization program for the apparent fear and avoidance of the commode. This, too, seemed to have minimal effect on bowel movements into the toilet, although he would readily sit on the toilet and not express any fear or anxiety.

Serendipitously, we discovered that the boy did not appear to know what muscles to use consciously in the act of defecation. Consequently, the parents and I set out to train the deficiencies in learning. Due to his occasional impaction, the physician had prescribed water irrigations to clean out his lower bowel. In the retraining procedure, we had the boy deliberately retain some of this water and then expel it. This procedure practiced the musculature so that eventually (in about 2 weeks of daily sessions) he learned the coordination needed for defecation into a diaper while awake and then into the toilet.

This case illustrates several aspects of pediatric psychological practice. First, for many clinical problems there is little or no existing literature on treatments. Second, multitheoretical approaches are frequently necessary, wherein the psychologist takes standard procedures and then individualizes the intervention for a patient's particular problem and situation or creates a unique treatment. Some ingenuity is involved, but sound psychological training also plays a major role, as the basic principles of behavior change and psychological interventions are always applicable and adaptable. The earlier story of Logan Wright's innovative approach to increasing children's fluid consumption evidences this point. Similarly, when the pediatric psychologist is confronted with each new problem, then assessment, conceptualization, and intervention follow sound psychological procedures. This occurs whether it is for unique presenting problems, such as a child's fear that her hand was shrinking (Waye, 1979) and a young boy's sexual fetish for women's bare feet (Shaw & Walker, 1979), or to more typical pediatric psychology cases of responding to the pain and anxiety of a burned child (Walker & Healy, 1980) and a child undergoing bone marrow aspiration (Hilgard & LeBaron, 1982). These more typical types of problems are exemplified in the cases in chapter 1.

Pediatric psychologists are not atheoretical, and many ascribe to one theory over others, but most practitioners are, by necessity, theoretically ambidextrous. A blind application of any technique is recognized as unlikely to be successful in all cases. Consequently, in the face of changing case conceptualizations, the pediatric psychologist may have to change, for example, the usual treatment protocol for tracheotomy addiction originally outlined by Wright, Nunnery, Eichel, and Scott (1968, 1969) and modified by Elliott and Olson (1982). Similarly, when presented with different case characteristics, Roberts and Ottinger (1979) modified the standardized encopretic treatment regimen described by Wright and Walker (1977).

This innovation and creativity is often necessary, as the practitioner employs a variety of theories and strategies. This facility produces a challenging aspect to pediatric psychology practice.

PRAGMATIC ORIENTATION

Implicit in the multitheoretical orientation of pediatric psychology is an emphasis on empiricism and pragmatism. Within ethical boundaries, if a procedure is demonstrably effective, regardless of its theoretical foundation, it will be used by practitioners facing urgent demands for timely remediation. As noted in an earlier section, the pediatrician and allied personnel have little time for lengthy drawn-out interventions with ill-defined outcomes. Many pediatricians expect pediatric psychologists to solve problems as rapidly and concisely as medical treatments typically do. An emphasis is also placed on observable or measurable changes.

In many cases, successful treatment is physically evident. For example, the child starts eating and gaining weight after treatment for a feeding disorder, the addicted child is finally able to tolerate withdrawal of the tracheotomy tube, and the child uses the toilet appropriately and stops soiling underpants with encopresis treatment. Other measurable data can indicate positive changes such as decreases in observed and self-reported medical fears, improvement on infant developmental indices upon comprehensive treatment for failure to thrive, and positive changes in teacher and parent ratings of hyperactivity after intervention.

Hence, the emphasis in pediatric psychology is on a *demonstration* of effectiveness. This pragmatic emphasis on results derives to some degree from the scientist-practitioner model of training, which many pediatric psychologists went through (or the heavier research emphasis of experimental and developmental psychologists who have become pediatric psychologists). Additionally, the general medical emphasis on "results" generates an orientation for pragmatism and accountability of interventions.

Also, as a consequence of this orientation, intellectual and developmental diagnostic evaluations tend to be more practical and less speculative regarding intrapsychic dynamics or personality characteristics (Walker, 1979a). Diagnostic reports and recommendations tend to be pragmatic and to the point, so that interventions are more likely to be implemented and accepted by physicians, staff, and parents. These are, therefore, more likely to be successful. Pediatric psychologists seek to use techniques that are more economical in terms of time and finances in addition to being more effective. This pragmatic emphasis often is tantamount to emphasizing behavioral techniques and short-term crisis intervention, but that is not always the case, as noted earlier.

DEVELOPMENTAL PERSPECTIVE

Since its inception, pediatric psychology has recognized the value of understanding developmental processes (Roberts, Maddux, & Wright, 1984; Tinsley & Parke, 1984). This developmental perspective has recently received renewed attention for psychopathology (Achenbach, 1982; Campbell, 1983) and therapy (Harris & Ferrari, 1983). Development refers to orderly changes over time. In relating the developmental process to pediatric psychology, these changes are relatively orderly, predictable, and measurable occurrences across the life span. The rapidity and extensiveness of the changes that occur in childhood make recognition and understanding of them imperative to those providing services to children and families.

Chronological age is one indicator of developmental change, but most practitioners find that age is, at best, a gross marker of developmental processes (e.g., physiological changes, experiences, cognitive abilities). Knowledge of child development is a fundamental component in clinical child and pediatric psychology training and practice (Maddux, Roberts, Sledden, & Wright, 1986; Roberts, Erickson, & Tuma, 1985; Roberts, Fanurik, & Elkins, in press). Thus, perhaps more than at any other period of life, developmental changes in biological–physical status, cognitive and intellectual ability, and psychosocial behavior need to be considered in diagnostic evaluation and therapeutic intervention (Roberts, Maddux, & Wright, 1984).

The developmental perspective in pediatric psychology requires some background in Piaget's cognitive development stages, Freud's and Erickson's personality and psychosocial development, Kohlberg's and Piaget's moral development, and Gesell's normative development (maturation and motoric behavior). Social learning theory also applies to developmental theory by postulating that the principles of learning are the same across all ages, whereas the specific content or behavior changes over time.

Finally, the developmental perspective in pediatric psychology has been applied to helping determine (a) when during the life span intervention and prevention services are most needed and for what kinds of problems, (b) when these services should be offered to maximize their efficacy and acceptance by the child and those responsible for the child, and (c) what types of services might be most effective (Roberts, Elkins, & Royal, 1984; Roberts, Maddux, & Wright, 1984).

TYPES OF CLINICAL CASES

Despite all the verbiage that can be written defining pediatric psychology practice, one characteristic more than anything else defines the field—the types of clinical cases evaluated and treated by the pediatric psychologist. The six cases beginning chapter 1 are just a small sampling of the variety of presenting problems. In chapter 4, various areas of intervention will be examined in more detail.

As one indication of the variety in practices, several tabulations have been compiled of problems referred to various pediatric psychology services. Table 2.1 is a compilation of several reports on parental concerns and common referral problems to pediatric psychology services. The problem categories were defined by Mesibov, Schroeder, and Wesson (1977). The differences in percentages for some of the problems probably result from the somewhat different emphases of the three units. As noted by Walker, Miller, and Smith (1985), the data from Walker (1979a) were collected in a pediatric psychology clinic serving a large children's hospital, whereas the Schroeder data were based on psychologists working in a private pediatricians' practice with a "call-in/come-in" component (Kanoy & Schroeder, 1985). Ottinger and Roberts (1980) tallied pediatricians' referrals to a

Table 2.1. Referral Problems to Three Pediatric Psychology Services

	% Referrals		
Problem	Kanoy & Schroeder (1985)[a]	Ottinger & Roberts (1980)	Walker (1979a)
Negative Behaviors (Toward parents)—doesn't obey, has tantrums, demanding, cries, whines.	15	10	10
Toileting Toilet training, encopresis, enuresis.	10	8	5
Developmental Delays Perceptual–motor problems, speech problems, slow development, school readiness, overactivity.	7	10	16[b]
School Problems Dislikes school, poor performance, reading or math problems, child aggression toward teacher.	9	15	9
Sleeping Problems Resists bedtime, nightmares, naps.	8	2	1
Personality Problems Lacks self-control, lacks motivation, irresponsible, overly lies, steals, dependent.	10	5	4
Sibling/Peer Problems Has no friends, aggressive toward peers and siblings, fighting.	7	1	<1
Divorce, Separation, Adoption Custody decisions, appropriate visitation schedule, how tell child.	8	1	2
Infant Management Feeding, nursing, cries all the time ("colic"), stimulation.	3	6	<1
Family Problems Mother feels isolated, conflict over discipline, parents arguing, child abuse.	4	3	10
Sex-Related Problems Opposite-sexed parent's clothing, no same-sexed friends, lack of sex-appropriate interests.	2	1	2
Food/Eating Problems Picky eater, eats too much or too little.	1	4	2
Specific Fears Dogs, trucks, dark.	2	—	<1
Specific Bad Habits Thumb sucking, nail biting, tics.	3	2	2
Parent's Negative Feelings Toward Child Dislikes child, no enjoyable interactions.	2	—	<1
Physical Complaints Headaches, stomachaches, fainting.	2	16	23
Parent's Concerns about School Is child getting what's needed, Does teacher understand child?	2	—	—
Moving Preparation for moving and problems of adjustment afterwards.	1	—	<1

Table 2.1. Referral Problems to Three Pediatric Psychology Services (continued)

	% Referrals		
Problem	Kanoy & Schroeder (1985)[a]	Ottinger & Roberts (1980)	Walker (1979a)
Death	1	—	1
Understanding and adjusting to death.			
Guidance of Talented Child	1	1	<1
Special programs, proper stimulation.			
Adjustment to Disease, Handicap	—	13	—
Drug/Alcohol Abuse	—	2	—
Miscellaneous	1	—	11[c]

Note. Blanks indicate category was not used in compilation. Percentages were rounded to nearest whole number.

[a] A totaled categorization based on Mesibov et al. (1977), Schroeder (1979), and new data in Kanoy and Schroeder (1985).

[b] Combines category with mental retardation and hyperactivity.

[c] Includes depression, hallucinations, suicide, instability.

pediatric psychology practicum in a clinical training program. Altogether, the problems and percentages illustrate the fairly consistent nature of pediatric psychology practice.

As can be seen, negative behaviors and school-related problems consistently comprise a high percentage of referral problems. Other more traditional clinical child psychology issues, such as personality problems, divorce, and family problems, are also highly represented. However, it should be noted, in all these services, that these were problems that presented via a medical referral mechanism. Thus, parents went to a physician first, even for problems that were clearly psychological and nonmedical. Most importantly, the table also shows the frequent referrals to pediatric psychologists for developmental delays, physical complaints, and a variety of other problems such as infant management and adjustment to disease or handicap. These types of cases typify the more usual problems thought of as characterizing pediatric psychological practice. That is, although problems common to clinical child psychology practice are seen in large numbers, the pediatric psychology practitioner also sees more problems associated with development and with physical health.

Of course, different services will vary in the frequencies of case categories. The compilation in Table 2.1 reflects general practices of pediatric psychology (mostly outpatient), whereas more specialized services (typically inpatient units) will have higher proportions of physical and health-related problems. Drotar (1977) found that in his inpatient consultation service of pediatric psychology about 30% of the referrals involved problems of management of chronic illness and adjustment or problems with burn, abuse, and accident victims. Close to 50% of the cases dealt with intellectual and developmental problems in association with chronic illness, deprivation, or language disabilities. Drotar further found that under 10% of his cases were for psychiatric or behavior problems.

Other even more specialized units of practice would have narrower ranges of referral problems. For example, psychologists working on a hematology–oncology unit deal more with pain management, adjustment to disease, medical noncompliance, and other problems. They would have many fewer cases of distinctly negative behaviors, school problems, or toileting problems, although these will frequently arise in conjunction with the medical conditions.

These percentages of common referral problems do not reflect the often novel and exciting cases that are presented to pediatric psychologists. It is perhaps these less frequent, but more quintessential pediatric psychology problems that truly indicate the special contribution pediatric psychology can make through innovation, creativity, and pragmaticism. It should be obvious that pediatric psychology relies heavily on clinical child psychological practices, while also providing more specialized applications related to children's health (Roberts, Fanurik, & Elkins, in press). Clinical cases typify pediatric psychology work more than do esoteric definitions. With these orientations as background, the actual roles and functions of pediatric psychology will be examined in the next chapters.

Chapter 3
Consultation with Pediatricians and Allied Personnel

Because of the type of problems presented and the nature of the referral mechanism through pediatrics, the practice of pediatric psychology typically developed more consultation–liaison relationships than did traditional clinical child psychology. The pediatric psychologist consults not only to parents, pediatricians, and medical staff, but also to school systems, to state and county welfare departments, to juvenile court systems, and to other health and social service agencies. Pediatricians and psychologists collaborate to respond to a variety of psychiatric, psychosomatic, developmental, learning, and other illness-related problems that are encountered in children's health care settings. The psychologist–pediatrician relationship is growing stronger, but given the two disciplines' diverse training and orientations noted in chapter 2, the liaison can be tenuous at times.

Differences such as mistrust or resentment of intrusions onto professional "turf," language or jargon differences, procedural differences, and, certainly, differences in knowledge bases, often interfere with effective functioning in collaboration. Despite these differences, the psychologist–pediatrician collaboration is thriving, is more often rewarding to each discipline, and, for the most part, is beneficial to patients. Actual consultation refers to the psychologist working with another professional or a parent rather than having direct contact with the child patient.

Pediatricians are calling on pediatric psychologists much as they might request consultation with another medical specialist, such as a dermatologist or cardiologist, depending on the particular problem. Of course, acceptance of the psychologist as a consultant, no matter the type of setting, will be contingent upon the provision of competent services, as it is and should be for other professional consultations. And this aspect should be uppermost in mind when one starts a pediatric psychology consultation practice.

Most of the factors important to the professional relationship are applicable to pediatric psychological practice in inpatient pediatric hospital services as well as hospital-based outpatient clinics and private pediatric clinics. Pediatricians, regardless of their work setting, serve as frontline health care professionals for a multitude of problems. Lee Salk (1969), an early pediatric psychologist, stated that a "pediatrician sees more human beings than any other professional during the most crucial stages of early development. . . . he is the first to be brought face to face with more developmental, learning, and emotional problems and has the greatest potential influence on child care practices" (p. 2). It is this frontline nature of pediatric practice that often draws in the consulting psychologist to make maximally effective interventions. The pediatrician will often call on the psychologist when facing a problem for which he or she has no training background and often no personal interest in treating.

In hospital practice, the request for psychological consultation often comes with a limit on time available to intervene (often same day attention is required) and a request for action on a specific problem (Drotar, Benjamin, Chwast, Litt, & Vajner, 1982; Walker et al., 1985). As noted in an earlier chapter, the emphasis in a referral is often on "action." In outpatient work, consultation requests may be both for immediate intervention and for longer-term strategies (Roberts & Wright, 1982). When the request for a "psych consult" is made, it may be for different levels of intensity of interaction ranging from a quick telephone call to slightly longer "curbside" or hallway discussions to more formal case workups of observation, testing, interviewing, and written reports. The psychologist may work with the child client or family for a direct psychological intervention, may work through the pediatrician and his or her staff to implement psychological services, or may work with a team of professionals each contributing to the overall treatment plan. In whatever the mode of consultation and intervention, the pediatric psychologist gears the strategy to the pediatric practice and the presenting problem. Indeed, the pediatric psychologist must have the ability to work flexibly in the various consultative relationships.

A number of conceptual models of pediatric consultation have been advanced (Burns & Cromer, 1978; Drotar, 1978; Stabler, 1979). Although the academic literature on the consultation process is large and growing, a model of applied consultation may be of more practical use for the pediatric psychology practitioner than systems analyses of consultation. With Logan Wright, I formulated such a consultation conceptualization that relies upon three models of consultation, with an overriding consultative orientation for pediatric psychology (Roberts & Wright, 1982). This conceptualization of consultation is applicable to the variety of medical settings for psychological practice. It is simple but also describes the complexity of psychologist–pediatrician liaisons.

Wright and I have labeled the three descriptive models of consultation: Independent Functions Model, Indirect Psychological Consultation Model, and Collaborative Team Model. In many ways, these models follow the models outlined by Stabler (1979) and Burns and Cromer (1978). The three basic relationship patterns interrelate. Any pediatric psychology consultantship may profitably involve any one of the three approaches, singly or in combination. I have not found that any particular arrangement is inherently better than the others, and many pediatric psychologists move from one model to another depending on the characteristics of the case or the referring pediatrician.

Underlying all three models is the concept that psychologists should provide services geared to the needs of the pediatrician and patients, wherever they are located. This may require some modification of consultation to fit the setting (inpatient or outpatient) and to fit the problem. The differing views of pediatric psychology require the individual psychologist to determine what are the functions of the consultantship—following his or her own proclivity and the demands of the particular setting. The psychologist can also adapt to the requirements of the situation by redefining his or her role in order to provide more effective services.

INDEPENDENT FUNCTIONS MODEL

When a consultation relationship follows this first pattern, the psychologist acts as a specialist who independently undertakes diagnosis and/or treatment of a patient referred by the pediatrician. Except for exchanges of information before and after referral of a patient, the pediatrician and psychologist work noncollaboratively. This pattern follows the usual establishment of independent practices of two professionals who make referrals to each other as needed. This model of the psychologist and pediatrician having independent functions has been noted by Drotar (1978) as a "noncollaborative" approach, and by Stabler (1979) as "coordination of multiservices."

The diagnostic role of this approach often relegates the psychologist to the role of tester, because many pediatricians hold the view that assessment is what psychologists do. In many cases, testing may not be needed, will have little impact on patient care, and may remove the psychologist from active participation in any therapeutic interventions. However, testing and diagnostic assessment constitute large portions of referrals in practice and, thus, are essential in consultation liaisons. Consequently, this aspect of practice requires some changes in many practices associated with clinical child psychology. For example, pediatricians, in both office and hospital practice, typically dislike reports and procedures filled, for example, with psychological jargon and speculation regarding intrapsychic dynamics.

Over the years, the role of the psychologist has greatly expanded from tester/diagnostician, so that treatment is now more often undertaken by the psychologist, especially in this independent functions consultation model. That is, the psychologist assumes major responsibility for developing and implementing an intervention for the presenting problem. However, when independently making pediatric psychological interventions with patients referred by pediatricians, the psychologist should be aware of several problems.

First, the psychologist should be careful not to "swallow" the patients up and totally remove participation and some aspects of decision making from the physician who initiated the referral. Indeed, totally removing responsibility and involvement from the primary-care physician who referred a patient rarely occurs in medical consultation practices. Thus, it would be arrogant and self-defeating to assume that psychologists should move patients away from the referring pediatricians. The pediatrician must be informed of what the psychologist is doing, just as the psychologist needs considerable knowledge of what the pediatrician is doing, especially when dealing with psychological problems related to medical disorders or treatment. Obviously, communication is needed—reports, letters, and telephone calls can help meet this requirement, if succinct and truly informative. A summary letter for the pediatrician's patient file can complete the consultation. Direct contact in conference meetings would be helpful, but often these are not possible, given the busy pediatric practice.

A second area of potential problems for the pediatric psychologist is that of "turf" issues. The psychologist often is functioning with problems or disorders traditionally considered the domain of the pediatrician. For example, the problem of encopresis (often called psychogenic constipation) responds to combinations of physical and behavioral interventions. Many pediatricians consider medical interventions most effective for encopresis and may resent psychologists' intrusions onto their turf when attempting to psychologically treat a problem that they may define as almost purely physical. Given psychologists' demonstrated success in treating encopresis, it is often too easy for the pediatric psychologist to take over treatment of both physical and behavioral aspects of an encopresis case and thereby take over the patient. Furthermore, the physics of enemas, mineral oil, and suppositories often used in the treatment of encopresis, as recommended by Wright (1973, 1975) and others, do not require medical prescription and may be bought over the counter. Yet, for a psychologist to recommend that a parent use these physics borders on medical prescribing, a privilege assiduously guarded by medical doctors, often more so than other procedures. The psychologist needs to recognize such concerns of the pediatrician a priori, but without "kowtowing" or employing less optimal procedures. Again, communication is critical, and a clear explanation of the procedures is necessary (perhaps relying on psychology-based articles published in the *medical* literature to back the psychologist, e.g., the article on encopresis published in *Clinical Pediatrics* by Wright & Walker, 1977). Thus, diplomatic education may take place to avoid resentment or resistance to psychologists' practicing on pediatric turf.

This independent functions consultation is probably the most prevalent form of consultation between pediatrician and psychologist because it follows a traditional pattern of independent professional practices assumed by both disciplines. Many nontraditional problems, however, can be handled in this model. The pediatrician makes a referral and continues to see a patient for medical treatment. The psychologist concurrently sees the patient or family and does what is needed in the psychological realm. The medical and behavioral management of juvenile diabetes for Amy (Case 4 in chapter 1) exemplifies this arrangement. Amy's pediatrician was concerned because she repeatedly failed to follow detailed instructions on diet, insulin injections, urine testing, and skin care (Lowe & Lutzker, 1979). This noncompliance resulted in a toxic condition, diabetic acidosis. The behavioral therapist met with Amy's pediatrician and family to review the regimen and the problems of noncompliance. Thereafter, the pediatrician set out the medically based instructions for diabetes treatment, while the psychological consultants designed a behavioral intervention for the noncompliance to the treatment regimen. Psychological techniques included a system of points contingent upon daily compliance and prompting memos about diet. Amy became highly consistent in fulfilling her responsibilities and evidenced fewer medical difficulties.

Other such independent functions consultation comes when the pediatrician sees a child who is having psychological problems concomitant to a medical disorder. These notably require special psychological interventions, and the pediatrician refers the patient to a psychologist. For example, a pediatrician referred a 14-year-old boy who had a 7-year history of encopresis (Roberts & Ottinger, 1979). He often went for days or weeks without a bowel movement. He soiled his underwear frequently. Although previous work with encopretics suggested that most encopretic children appear free of psychopathology, this young man exhibited several problems in interpersonal relationships and academic functioning. The encopresis and the social difficulties seemed to be based in his high level of anxiety.

In this case, the pediatrician and psychologist undertook independent functions on different aspects of the problems. The pediatrician designed a primary medical treatment for the encopresis symptoms, including enemas, suppositories, and mineral oil to insure a daily bowel movement and to restore muscle tone to the bowel. These were phased out over time. The psychological intervention consisted of a multifaceted behavioral treatment comprising training in progressive muscle relaxation, in self-management skills (e.g., for school work), and in social and assertion skills. Over time the patient established a daily bowel habit with notable decreases in nervousness in many previously arousing situations. His grades improved and he appeared to withdraw less from social situations. In this case, although there was discussion between the pediatrician and the therapist, each worked fairly independently because their foci were distinct. The pediatrician attended to the encopresis manifestations, and the psychologist focused on the behavioral factors that probably influenced the encopresis.

Parents frequently turn to the family physician or pediatrician when confronting a psychologically related problem with their child because most have had no prior relationship with the mental health establishment. The physician is a continuing contact who is knowledgeable and interested and who can help parents find the most appropriate mental health professional. In many cases of independent consultation, the pediatrician may become aware of some problems sooner than other professionals and may also request traditional psychological therapy or assessment (e.g., testing for learning disabilities; divorce counseling for the children). In these types of cases the pediatrician may not require much interactive consultation or collaboration because the problem is more clearly outside the pediatric/medical realm than are many other presenting disorders in the pediatric psychology arena.

The pediatric psychologist and pediatrician can function effectively in this independent practice arrangement as long as they maintain appropriate communication and mutual respect for each other's expertise. This role may be restrictive if the psychologist permits it. The pediatrician may consider only some types of cases to be appropriate for referral, and, as a consequence, the psychologist's role will be limited. For example, if the pediatrician views the role of diagnostician or tester as the main one for psychologists, then that will be what is received in the way of referrals. The pediatrician may see psychology as having utility only for behavioral problems at home or at school and make referrals only for these (e.g., noncompliance with teachers or parents, learning disabilities). Thus, the pediatrician would not see value in referring patients and families whose behavior problems are associated with medical conditions (e.g., noncompliance with medical regimens). Certainly, this type of restrictive pediatrician would not refer patients whose medical condition is amenable to psychological intervention (e.g., encopresis, tracheotomy addiction). In this situation, there also is probably no active input or education by the psychologist in the definition of functions for psychologists. Consequently, the psychologist may need to educate the physician about psychological roles beyond the diagnostic roles and behavioral disorders and more about what are appropriate referrals of additional problems.

INDIRECT PSYCHOLOGICAL
CONSULTATION MODEL

The second approach to a consultation arrangement is one in which the pediatrician retains the major responsibility for patient management. The psychologist works with the pediatrician who provides psychosocial services to the patient and family. The psychologist has no or limited contact with the actual client and usually considers only data gathered by the pediatrician. Thus, the psychological service is indirectly provided by the psychologist. This pediatric/psychological relationship is more collaborative than the independent functions model outlined in the previous section. This second type of consultation usually develops in medical center settings that also may have a teaching function (e.g., the psychologist supervises a pediatric resident) because the relative positions of consultee–

consultant often require an educative stance of teacher–learner rather than a true collaboration between "equals" in the professions.

This consultation model may increase in frequency over time given the new medical emphasis for primary care practitioners to provide many mental health-oriented services. Thus, it may be likely that more pediatricians currently practicing will request psychological assistance of such an educational/supervisory nature. The pediatrician, in turn, would carry through on behavioral interventions for various problems. This model of indirect psychological contact with patients is similar to the models labeled "process-educative" (Stabler, 1979) and a combination of "didactic/seminar," "supervision," and "client-centered (case) consultation" from Burns and Cromer (1978).

This psychologist-consultant arrangement can take several forms. The pediatrician may request brief contact (e.g., by telephone call) for specific information. The brief contact may also come, if the psychologist is available, in "on-the-spot" consultations for particular problems. These brief contacts may involved questions of: (a) the appropriateness of a child behavior and possible treatments (e.g., bedwetting at age 6 years); (b) the interpretation of test data (e.g., school achievement test scores); (c) community sources of assistance (e.g., for special education classes or tutoring); and (d) appropriateness of a referral (e.g., what psychology can do for an emotionally disturbed mentally retarded child). The psychologist may answer these questions briefly or suggest a more detailed examination.

A second form of indirect psychological consultation can occur through the presentation of information in seminars, conferences, pediatric section meetings, and inservice training or continuing education programs for pediatricians, nurses, and staff. Many psychologists setting up new consultation services in pediatric settings have found these activities very fruitful for advertising their availability and for instructing in basic psychosocial approaches (Drotar, 1982). This form of consultation is not oriented to a specific case, but more to general psychological approaches. It can enhance the overall effectiveness of the pediatrician and improve the psychosocial care of pediatric patients and their families. The psychologist may never actually see the recipients of these "indirect" psychological interventions.

A third indirect patient treatment approach can occur when a mutual trust has developed about the other professional's abilities. In this approach, the pediatrician would carry out a specified psychosocial intervention recommended by the psychologist-consultant, who would have no direct patient contact. For example, as elaborated later in this chapter, standardized procedures can be established for certain types of behavioral disorders frequently appearing in pediatric practice. Edward Christophersen, a pediatric psychologist, has designed a number of protocols or guidelines that pediatricians or nursing staff might use for a variety of problems. For example, he prepared sets of guidelines for clinicians and for parents on how to handle temper tantrums and bedtime crying or resistance

Table 3.1. Protocols for Assessment and Treatment

Problem	Available In
Toilet training	Azrin & Foxx, 1974 Christophersen & Rapoff, 1983
Encopresis treatment	Christophersen & Rainey, 1976 Christophersen & Rapoff, 1983 Wright & Walker, 1977
Daily progress chart for assessment of urinary and fecal incontinence	Varni, 1983
Dry bed training	Azrin & Besalel, 1979 Azrin, Sneed, & Foxx, 1974
Encourage child safety seat use	Christophersen & Gyulay, 1981
Bedtime problems	Christophersen, 1982 Rainey & Christophersen, 1976 Wright, Woodcock, & Scott, 1970
Temper tantrums	Christophersen, 1982 Rainey & Christophersen, 1976
General child behavior management	Christophersen, 1977, 1982 Forehand & McMahon, 1981
Behavior problems away from home	Drabman & Jarvie, 1977 Drabman & Rosenbaum, 1980
Child behavior at supermarkets	Barnard, Christophersen, & Wolf, 1977
Early morning dawdling	Christophersen, 1982 Drabman & Rosenbaum, 1980
Teaching dressing	Christophersen, 1982
Mealtime problems	Christophersen, 1982 Forehand & McMahon, 1981
Food and beverage intake record	Varni, 1983
Training pill swallowing	Funk, Mullins, & Olson, 1984
Pain diary	McGrath, 1983 Richardson, McGrath, Cunningham, & Humphreys, 1983
Methods of improving pediatric medical compliance	Jones, 1983
Children's fear survey	Walker, 1979a
Children's reinforcement survey	Cautela & Brion-Meisels, 1979 Phillips, Fischer, & Singh, 1977

(Christophersen & Rainey, 1976). These authors suggest that these protocols can be used by nurse clinicians in pediatric settings. Additional protocols are noted later in this chapter. (See Table 3.1.)

In other indirect psychological consultation, the psychologist may provide overview and ready availability in consulting on behaviorally based interventions with enuresis or encopresis that feasibly can be made by pediatricians and their staffs. In the case of Joey, the encopretic boy (Case 3 in chapter 1), the medical diagnosis was made in the pediatric clinic and hospital. The behavioral intervention of rewards (lollipops, mother's praise, and play periods with his parents at night) for appropriate toileting in combination with a regimen of mineral oil could be easily implemented by the pediatrician with overview by a consulting psychologist (Roberts et al., 1977).

Christophersen and Rapoff (1983) present a set of treatment instructions for parents and practitioners that can be used for encopresis cases. Similarly, standardized procedures can also be established for a pediatric practice to deal with relatively common problems such as psychogenic pain or anxiety associated with medical events. Intervention by the pediatrician for these types of patients' problems may be more acceptable and effective than directly involving the psychologist, because the parents and the child may be more willing to accept the pediatrician's psychosocial advice for a problem they view as a physical one. Thus, indirect consultation may be particularly useful for cases where the psychologist's presence would engender particular resistance. Most mental health professionals have received the type of referral I have, for a consultation regarding a medical inpatient, only to enter the hospital room and hear the parent or child say, "I don't need a shrink. The problem's a real medical one, not in the head." Often, better preparation by the attending physician for such mental health consultation would ease this referral, but it may be as appropriate to instruct the physician and nursing staff to make the psychosocial interventions.

These three forms of indirect patient contact may be present in various ways of psychological consulting to pediatric practices. However, some restrictions may arise on this indirect approach. First, the consulting psychologist may not actually see the patient and must rely on diagnostic data gathered by the pediatrician. Problems with the type and reliability of this assessment can impede accurate, effective decision making or recommendations on the part of the psychologist called to consult. Consequently, the psychologist may need to teach the pediatrician some assessment skills and provide appropriate evaluation devices. This often includes interviewing skills and psychosocial questioning, which are not a major component in the typical physician's repertoire.

The educative process requires considerable diplomacy in how it is presented. Rather than lecture to the pediatrician, a tack usually lacking tact, I have found it useful to summarize background information from the literature, diagnostic questions, and brief treatment recommendations in one- or two-page handouts. These can be given to the pediatrician to provide to the parent or child and the pediatric staff. At the same time, the material does get in front of the pediatrician's eyes. Unloading a stack of books or articles on the pediatrician's desk is unlikely to have much utility, whereas the briefing sheets can be readily assimilated. Nonetheless, the psychologist's natural concern for quality and efficacy of treatment in this manner may limit indirect consultation.

A second problem comes if resentment develops in the pediatrician because he or she perceives this role as subservient to the psychologist. On the other hand, the psychologist may resent relinquishing some cherished aspects of psychological practice, namely, diagnosis and treatment. Another problem arises, similar to the pediatrician's potential resentment of the psychologist's intrusion into the pediatric turf, wherein the psychologist views negatively the pediatrician's assuming more of the roles of the mental health practitioner. In this view, giving over too many psychological techniques threatens the psychologist's practice. A final problem is very likely to arise with this mode of psychological services: The pediatrician may not be interested in personally providing the actual service and may not have the time needed to learn and implement it. Thus, training and consulting to support personnel such as nurses, pediatric nurse practitioners, and even clerical staff may be necessary.

COLLABORATIVE TEAM MODEL

The third major model of psychological consulting to the pediatrician is one of true collaboration. In this approach, the pediatrician and psychologist work together with shared responsibility and joint decision making. Case management is conducted conjointly, with the professionals contributing their own unique perspectives and competence. Often in this approach, roles may not be clearly demarcated in the provision of any one particular service, although some division of responsibility is necessary. A cooperative team is, thus, at the essence of this type of pediatrician–psychologist consulting. In many ways, this model is similar to the models of "process consultation" (Stabler, 1979) and "collaboration" (Burns & Cromer, 1978).

This model represents an ideal situation where professionals coact as functional equals. The team approach of collaboration is more likely to exist in special units or within institutions, such as teams consulting to hospital sections of oncology, renal dialysis, surgery, or neonatal intensive care. In such settings, teams of social workers, medical doctors, psychologists, clergy, audiologists and speech pathologists, educational experts, and others can collaborate with a common goal of using all resources to benefit the patient.

Such teams are less likely in the private pediatric practice away from teaching/ research centers. This decreased likelihood is due to the demands of practice that require more independent functioning. Financial restraints and availability of allied resources also limit such services. Though it is unfortunate that the typical pediatric office practice rarely has extensive personnel resources, several types of problems can be treated with only the psychologist and limited pediatric staff. Additionally, more psychologists are affiliating with larger pediatric clinics and also associating with social workers and educational specialists for their services. Although such team collaboration is increasing in the private practice of pediatrics, interdisciplinary teams are more frequently found in larger hospitals and medical centers.

Numerous problems that require a psychological and medical coalition are amenable to this conjoint approach (e.g., obesity, anorexia nervosa, drug abuse, physical handicaps, and chronic diseases), with each team member focusing on different aspects. In the case of anorexia nervosa, for example, the extensive weight loss and accompanying problems (e.g., gastric hypoacidity, carotenemia, hypoproteinimia) are medical concerns. Aspects of medical treatment include monitoring these problems as well as prescribing an appropriate diet. The psychologist, in conjunction with the pediatrician's interventions, can establish behavioral contingencies for eating and weight gain while working with the patient in psychotherapy for increasing self-perceptions of trust and self-control. Collaboration or jointly coordinated interventions are necessary with this life-threatening condition. Such necessity of joint work precludes an independent functions model of consultation.

As another example of collaborative team work, a chronic disease such as juvenile diabetes requires continual medical overview for diet, insulin intake, urinalysis, and exercise. The consulting psychologist may assist in enhancing the patient's compliance to the medical regimen and in the patient's adjustment to the disease itself. This psychological work requires extensive knowledge of the pediatrician's treatment approach and a dialogue on appropriate regimens, thus precluding an independent functions practice. The indirect consultation approach may work in some instances if the pediatrician is prepared and interested in spending the time and making the effort for the psychosocial counseling. In all likelihood, a collaborative team model works best where both medical and psychological involvement is required that cannot be transferred to any other professional.

As an example of the collaborative approach, a child with cerebral palsy required psychological intervention consisting of counseling, relaxation training, and self-monitoring to increase her muscle-stretching exercises (which she tried to avoid). Meanwhile, the medical aspects of the case were continually checked by the conferring pediatrician and the physical therapist (La Greca & Ottinger, 1979).

Developmental problems, which need different resources in a team approach, also occur frequently (Walker, 1979a). The failure-to-thrive case of Oscar (Case 1 in chapter 1) demonstrates the collaboration of psychologists, pediatric nurse practitioners, physicians, social workers, and occupational therapists (Roberts & Horner, 1979). The psychologists' inputs to this alliance were developmental assessment of the child, interventions to increase food intake by the child and to increase the parents' stimulation of the boy, and cognitive-behavioral treatment of the mother's depression. The physician and pediatric nurse practitioner provided comprehensive health care, and the occupational therapists worked on psychomotor stimulation of Oscar. Social workers in the hospital assisted in finding financial resources for better housing and nutrition.

Interdisciplinary resources usually exist in the hospital or community even if not directly part of the pediatric section of a hospital or office practice. The psychologist's role may be to locate and to coordinate the various services for particular patients as the need arises. Such teams for collaboration may be needed on an ad hoc basis, although in many settings established team structures exist to facilitate conjoint functioning. Structural interdisciplinary teams have been working well in university-affiliated facilities (UAFs), often under the various names of child study center (e.g., University of Oklahoma Health Sciences Center), child evaluation clinic (e.g., University of Louisville Medical Center), and child development center (e.g., Georgetown University Medical Center). However, these settings for collaborative teams require extensive resources and have a large focus. Other teams develop in response to intensive needs on a particular unit for the variety of coordinated services only a team can provide (e.g., pediatric oncology, dialysis, or burn wards).

Another major area for collaborative team efforts is community prevention programming (Roberts & Peterson, 1984a, 1984b). These types of collaborative services have been relatively untouched by pediatric psychologists. Nevertheless, psychologists could serve as consultants to teams consisting of several professionals interested in improving children's health care. Such efforts might include assisting disease immunization programs, encouraging proper nutrition and/or breast feeding to alleviate infant mortality, psychologically preparing children for physical examinations or dental checkups, screening school children for mental and physical health problems, and child abuse screening and follow-up. Psychologists have particular interests and expertise to bring to these efforts that may get underrecognized and underutilized unless one gets involved and demonstrates the usefulness of psychology. For example, research psychologists have gotten involved with finding ways to motivate parents to bring their children in for inoculations (e.g., Yokley & Glenwick, 1984). These psychology-based interventions include evaluating prompts and reminders (e.g., postcards, phone calls) and contingent rewards for keeping appointments to get immunizations. This collaborative work utilizes psychology's often unique research and program evaluation skills to find the most cost-effective interventions.

Burns and Cromer (1978) note that the collaborative approach allows the pediatrician to share responsibility for many mental health interventions. The conjoint consultative relationship encourages reciprocal respect for the unique contributions of each profession. However, the collaborative team approach is not without limitations and has been criticized for compartmentalizing patients, families, and problems. In a valuable description of personal experiences, Robert and Peggy Stinson (1983) have written about their son's premature birth and the subsequent 6 months of invasive and debilitating medical treatments until his death (Roberts, 1985). Among many criticisms of various professionals' actions and attitudes, the Stinsons call into question the professional interdisciplinary team:

I think there are too many people in the room. (p. 48)

I really resent the fact that you can't ask for a doctor without having a "team" show up, each member of which is there to take care of one aspect of our "problem." I don't like being "dealt with." Probably I'm reading too much into the voice by "hearing" them assemble and then seeing them arrive together to deal with us. It's patronizing and gives the impression of something hidden and unequal between us. (p. 70)

Greater sensitivity to patients and parents can perhaps remedy the unfortunate result of the collaborative team approach as experienced by the Stinsons. In many other cases, this type of team can provide much needed and beneficial support to the families and patients. The challenge of working with other professionals, given their different backgrounds and conceptualizations, remains an opportunity for the pediatric psychologist to contribute special qualities.

PEDIATRIC PRACTICE
CONSULTATION ORIENTATION

Regardless of which of the three consultation approaches or combinations is followed, there are numerous exciting ways the pediatric psychologist can function to enhance the pediatrician's practice in hospital or office. Thus, the psychologist consultant need not feel constrained into any one of these models. Overriding all three models is often the psychologist's orientation to the particular needs of the pediatrician and actual medical practice. In this way, the psychologist can assume an active and vital role in consulting to the practicing pediatrician, while maintaining a distinct professional identity as a health-care provider.

When psychologists help solve the pediatricians' problems, they enhance the physicians' reputations as well as their own. The former effect is likely to open many more opportunities for service and research. Pediatricians usually recognize the patients' needs and want to provide more comprehensive services, but time constraints often do not permit their direct participation. In particular, for the private practitioner, time is money (as, indeed, it is for the practicing psychologist). The pediatric psychologist is most likely to succeed in gaining acceptance if the programs proposed require little of the pediatrician's time, but do have a significant impact on patient care.

Although I acknowledge that psychologists have a need for a distinct professional identity, the pediatric psychologist is in a unique position vis-à-vis medicine that may, at times, require subordination of that need in order to practice and to provide better health care of children. Consequently, many consultation efforts are superficially directed less at increasing the psychologists' roles and more at enhancing the pediatricians' practice. This type of work does not diminish the value of psychology's contributions to the health-care field. However, a clear orientation to meeting the needs of pediatric practice and the needs of children can be exhibited in several ways.

Psychosocial Screening

The psychologist, in establishing a consultantship, may find it useful to work with the pediatrician in screening mental health problems. Because the pediatrician sees many children at critical periods of development, it is logical that the pediatric practice serve as a first line for identifying children with problems. Screening is a concept already familiar to pediatricians, that is, the separation of patients on the basis of key indicators of medical problems (e.g., routine blood tests of newborns for phenylketonuria). Data gathered in screening procedures are considered indicative of problems, not totally diagnostic; in-depth follow-up examination is usually required when an indication of a disorder is observed. Following an algorithm-screening approach, some pediatricians also use protocols for managing telephone calls for medical complaints such as fevers, upper respiratory infections, head injury, abdominal pain, and other frequently phoned-in complaints. These procedures help screen the calls, improve the patient management, and standardize data gathering (Nelson, Vaughan, & McKay, 1975).

The pediatrician has already been trained in some psychosocial screening procedures. For example, most have had experience with the Denver Developmental Screening Test (DDST: Frankenburg, Fandal, Sciarillo, & Burgess, 1981), which serves as a first assessment of an infant's developmental status. Should delayed development be found on the DDST, referral for a comprehensive psychological evaluation would then rely upon a more diagnostic instrument, such as the Bayley Scales of Infant Development (see chapter 4).

Additional psychological screening procedures may need to be added to the pediatrician's armamentarium. For example, a general psychological portion has been developed for the Pediatric Multiphasic Examination (Allen & Shinefield, 1974; Metz, Allen, Barr, & Shinefield, 1976). The various sections of this examination for children ages 4 to 16 years are used to screen children for psychological problems, with referral for more intensive diagnostic testing and treatment. Other screening techniques under development are aimed at specific disorders such as identifying infants "at risk" for child abuse, failure to thrive, or developmental disorders and for social or school adjustment problems. Models of medical screening protocols often use flowchart designs with branching questions. Pediatric psychologists may find it useful to adapt these types of protocols for a large number of common behavioral problems (for both telephoned and office-referred complaints).

Furthermore, the psychologist can help the pediatrician make timely and appropriate referrals for psychological intervention. The psychologist does not want to be overwhelmed by referrals for every child with a possible problem, because many children are potentially identifiable as such. Thus, the pediatrician and psychologist can jointly establish a decision-making framework for determining which cases the pediatrician will handle, which ones need psychological supervision of the pediatrician, and which will be referred to the psychologist.

Protocols and Checklists for Assessment and Treatment

The psychologist can provide protocols, checklists, and questionnaires to the pediatrician to assist (a) in screening and referral and (b) in implementing standardized treatment procedures. In the first instance, the use of one- or two-page assessment devices can identify potential problems rapidly through interviews by pediatric staff or parental completion of the forms. These diagnostic and treatment protocols might follow the format of an algorithm, as noted earlier. The pediatrician should already have some protocols as standard practice for determining the child's growth in comparison to norms on growth curves (height, weight, head circumference: National Center for Health Statistics Growth Charts, 1976; Nelson et al., 1975; Wright, 1979b). When I first introduced a protocol to a new family medicine physician, I found that comparing the psychological protocols to the existing medical ones helped in gaining his acceptance of the additional procedures for screening and referral.

The psychologist may recommend assessment protocols already well-established in psychological settings (the Adaptive Behavior Rating Scale, Parenting Stress Index, the Personality Inventory for Children). Significant developmental milestones can also be charted following the Gesell Developmental Schedules or through other examinations of neurodevelopmental progress. Results from these sorts of scales are useful for identifying the developmentally delayed child and for requesting a comprehensive evaluation. Some checklists are also useful for suggesting when to begin developmental interventions (e.g., toilet training: Azrin & Foxx, 1974). The psychologist will want to maintain considerable control over use and interpretation of these protocols.

Other standardized scales or protocols may be more diagnostic or predictive, such as those quantifying the degree of hyperactivity (Barkley, 1981; Conners, 1969), determining child abuse (Friedman, Sandler, Hernandez, & Wolfe, 1981), assessing childhood behavioral disorders (Achenbach, 1978; Atkeson & Forehand, 1981), evaluating learning disabilities (Katz, 1984), and assessing fears and phobias (Barrios, Hartmann, & Shigetomi, 1981).

The pediatric psychologist may wish to investigate referral protocols and checklists that are still under development, but show promise. For example, Wright (1978a) presents several checklists based on reviews of the literature. Similarly, the consulting psychologist may choose to develop particular checklists for the pediatrician. For example, if the patient population comes from a poor or older neighborhood, lead poisoning from old paint chips may be a significant concern. An examination of the literature will reveal important psychological features of lead poisoning and circumstances leading to it. A lead poisoning protocol for psychological concomitants can supplement the medical tests the pediatrician may utilize. Other protocols may be needed for assessing children's eating disorders, school problems, habits and compulsions, or any number of potential disorders that are seen with any frequency in the specific pediatric setting.

In all cases, the psychologist must be cautious in supplying screening and preliminary diagnostic instruments to the pediatric staff without appropriate psychological consultation and supervision. Ultimate responsibility to ensure that these procedures are used properly rests with the psychologist.

A second way protocols can be used for enhancing pediatric practice is in the implementation of standardized treatment procedures. As noted earlier, the pediatrician and auxiliary staff can conduct many psychological interventions with the consultation of the pediatric psychologist by following a previously designed course of action. The use of established procedures permits the controlled treatment by staff or parents for problems that recur frequently. The procedures can include branching decision-making trees for when changes in treatment programs should be made to individualize the intervention or when problems arise. Christophersen and Rapoff (1980) suggest condensing treatment procedures for behavior problems into protocols of one or two pages.

The advantage of standardized procedure protocols is that they are immediately present and can be instituted during the presenting clinic visit. Logan Wright (1980) has described the use of such protocols as the means of providing standardized compliance procedures. A protocol provides (a) a rationale and procedure for the intervention and any necessary compliance, (b) a standardized mechanism for delineating and recording interactions between the patient or the parent and the practitioner, (c) a means for evaluating and improving the degree of compliance, and (d) a structuring of the involvement of the practitioner.

When working on toilet training, for example, the psychologist or pediatrician can provide parents a copy of *Toilet Training in Less Than a Day* (Azrin & Foxx, 1974), and checklists can be drawn from the book for staff to monitor parental actions and child progress (e.g., Christophersen & Rapoff, 1983; Walker, 1978). The consulting psychologist may wish to utilize treatment protocols for such pediatric psychological problems as encopresis, behavioral noncompliance, anorexia nervosa, medication regimen compliance, obesity, juvenile diabetes, asthma, and many other frequent referral problems.

These protocols may be of benefit in organizing the pediatrician's staff and in monitoring the behavior of patients and parents. Brief intervention protocols or brochures for parents can be prepared for simpler problems as well. Table 3.1 presents a number of problems for which protocols have been developed and published.

The type of standardized psychological interventions suggested here should be employed primarily for fairly simple and circumscribed problems. The psychologist should maintain some control to insure appropriateness of application. As a form of consultation to the pediatric practice, however, standardized procedures have the advantages of cost-efficiency by (a) minimizing pediatrician and psychologist time through the use of existing staff, (b) being effective, (c) providing needed services, and (d) allowing the psychologist to focus on more complicated psychological cases. The kinds of treatment protocols developed will depend on the needs of the clinic practice and the particular needs of the individual patients. Christophersen and Rapoff (1980) note that when the psychologist provides treatment protocols, they need to be readily incorporable, with a minimum disruption, into the existing practice, and they need to be cost-efficient.

Reading for Pediatricians, Parents, and Children

The psychologist can assist the pediatrician to competently handle some situations through a bibliographic approach. Many books and articles are available commercially for parents and children and professionally for pediatricians. The psychologist can help the pediatrician wade through the overwhelming number of books, recommending those that the parents can read for their own education or that the child can read or be read to in order to help enhance adjustment and understanding of a particular problem or situation. Most importantly, the psychologist can use readings to educate and prepare the pediatrician in several psychological areas.

Numerous questions arise in pediatric practice that often are referred to as "Dr. Spock" or "one-hand-on-the-door" questions (Wright, 1979a). These are the general types of questions asked of a pediatrician (and often of a psychologist) that are seemingly offhand, but indicate a parent's need for information. I have also heard of the "by the way, doctor" questions. These questions include: "When and how do I start toilet training?" "Is it normal for a 10-month-old boy to hold his breath until he turns blue?" "Is it right for a little girl to play with her genitals?" David MacPhee (1984), a psychologist, has developed an interesting list of these common developmental issues asked of pediatricians. I have found it valuable to go through the list to determine some answers a priori and generate discussions with medical residents to increase their knowledge of child development issues.

These questions often do not lend themselves to 5 or 10 minutes of advice. Having protocols on hand as previously described would obviously help in this situation. However, there is little likelihood that all possible questions can be prepared for in advance. What can be done is to provide bibliotherapeutic assistance. Parents can be given books to read or told where to acquire books and asked to return for extended consultation if they need additional assistance. (I call local bookstores to request that certain books be available, with the assurance that I would refer my clients to their stores to buy the stock.)

Sometimes parents request information regarding specific psychological/ behavioral problems. As detailed in Table 3.2, some excellent self-help books directed at parents are available for a number of problems. In many cases, this type of information should not take the place of an involved professional, but can be complementary to the professional's educative and treatment efforts.

An additional role the pediatric psychologist and pediatrician can take is in providing readings to children on subjects with which they are concerned. A profitable approach to children's adjustment or understanding is to provide fictional or biographical storybooks that deal realistically with problems. A regular feature of the *Journal of Clinical Child Psychology* is a section containing annotated bibliographies and reviews of books on specific topics for children and parents (e.g., *Sexuality Education*, Schroeder, Gordon, & McConnell, 1984a; *Divorce*, Schroeder et al., 1984b; *Learning Disabilities*, Schroeder et al., 1985). *Clinical Pediatrics* also publishes a regular column on children's books for selected topics with annotations on the content and age appropriateness. Topics have included death (Grossman, 1983a), divorce (Grossman, 1983b), adoption (Grossman, 1983c), alcoholism (Grossman, 1983d), fear of medical treatments (Grossman, 1984a), attitudes about handicaps (Grossman, 1984b), sex education (Grossman, 1984c), and prolonged illness (Grossman, 1985). Other resources list good books and research for distribution by the consulting psychologist (e.g., physically handicapped children: Van Vechten, Satterwhite, & Pless, 1977; death: Aradine, 1976).

The psychologist can further educate the pediatrician by preparing a brief reading curriculum on particular problems for the pediatrician and staff. Lewis (1978), for example, provides a list of references for professionals on terminal illness, grief, developmental changes in perceptions, reactions by parents, and professionals' own reactions to terminal illness. These types of reading lists are likely to be most appreciated when the physician is dealing extensively with a particular type of patient or when he or she expresses an interest in becoming more familiar with the psychosocial aspects of some pediatric problems. Table 3.2 lists several resources that may be useful in a bibliotherapeutic approach by the pediatrician or psychologist.

Table 3.2. Bibliotherapy

The following books may be useful to have available in pediatric and pediatric psychology practices on selected topics. (See the reference list for complete bibliographic information.)
For Parents
General child management and parenting
  Becker, *Parents are Teachers*, 1971.
  Christophersen, *Little People*, 1977.
  Patterson & Gullion, *Living with Children*, 1968.
  Wright, *Parent Power*, 1981.
General pediatric issues
  Simon & Cohen, *The Parent's Pediatric Companion*, 1985.
  Spock & Rothenberg, *Dr. Spock's Baby and Child Care*, 1985.   (continued)

Learning disabilities
  Osman, *No One to Play With: The Social Side of Learning Disabilities*, 1982.
Cancer
  Adams & Deveau, *Coping with Childhood Cancer,* 1984.
Anxiety & fears
  Wolman, *Children's Fears*, 1978.
Toilet training
  Azrin & Besalel, *A Parent's Guide to Bedwetting Control*, 1979.
  Azrin & Foxx, *Toilet Training in Less Than a Day,* 1974.
Divorce
  Anderson & Anderson, *Mom and Dad are Divorced, But I'm Not*, 1981.
  Salk, *What Every Child Would Like His Parents to Know About Divorce*, 1978.
Sex education
  Gordon & Gordon, *Raising a Child Conservatively in a Sexually Permissive World*, 1983.
For Children
Anxiety & fears
  Blume, *It's Not the End of the World*, 1972.
  Fassler, *The Boy with a Problem*, 1972.
Divorce
  Gardner, *The Boys and Girls Book About Divorce*, 1970.
  Hazen, *Two Homes to Live In*, 1983.
  Magid & Schreibman, *Divorce Is . . . A Kid's Coloring Book*, 1980.
  Sinberg, *Divorce is a Grown-Up Problem*, 1979.
Handicaps
  Adams, *Like It Is: Facts and Feeling About Handicaps From Kids Who Know,* 1974.
  Fassler, *Howie Helps Himself*, 1975.
  Harries, *They Triumphed Over Their Handicaps*, 1981.
  Levine, *Lisa and her Soundless World*, 1974.
Mental retardation & learning disabilities
  Fassler, *One Little Girl*, 1969.
  Hayes, *The Tuned-In, Turned-on Book About Learning Problems*, 1974.
  Lynch, *Mary Fran and Mo*, 1979.
  Sobol, *My Brother Steven is Retarded*, 1977.
Sex education
  Brooks, *So That's How I was Born!* 1983.
  Gordon, *Girls are Girls and Boys are Boys, So What's the Difference?* 1983.
  Gruenberg, *The Wonderful Story of How You Were Born*, 1970.
  Sheffield, *Where Do Babies Come From?* 1973.
Death
  Bernstein & Gullo, *When People Die*, 1977.
  Brown, *The Dead Bird*, 1958.
  Krementz, *How It Feels When a Parent Dies*, 1981.
  Viorst, *The Tenth Good Thing About Barney,* 1972.
  White, *Charlotte's Web,*1952.
Hospitalization
  Cilotta & Livingston, *Why Am I Going to the Hospital?* 1981.
  Howe, *The Hospital Book*, 1981.
Fears
  Bonsall, *Who's Afraid of the Dark?* 1980.
  Stanek, *Who's Afraid of the Dark?* 1980.
Chronic Illness
  Hermes, *What If They Knew?* 1980 (epilepsy).
  Jones, *Angie and me*, 1981 (arthritis).
  Roy, *Where's Buddy?* 1982 (diabetes).
  Sachs, *Just Like Always*, 1981 (scoliosis).

The practitioner needs to maintain some overview of the quality of the books provided in this approach. There are many books on a variety of psychological topics for children and parents that are misleading in the information presented, are inappropriate for specific contexts, and may produce undesirable side effects. Peterson (1984a), for example, reviewed a book for parents on pregnancy, birth, and early infancy that contained some serious inaccuracies regarding fetal nutrition, did not contain some necessary material, and seemed to raise negative expectations for child rearing.

In my work with hospital preparation materials, I have examined many commercially available books that are designed to prepare a child for hospitalization. Many of these do not adequately do the job, and some also contain potentially harmful features. There are many myths perpetuated by these books. For example, some preparation materials tell the child that injections feel like mosquito bites and that blood tests in the finger or arm do not hurt "at all." Several booklets prepare children for tonsillectomies by emphasizing that after surgery the child will get all the ice cream he or she wants. These books fail to acknowledge truthfully that there is any discomfort. One book describes a child walking into a room where a nurse and a man are waiting dressed in green. They lift the girl onto a table, and she blows up a balloon and falls asleep. Another book depicts a child walking hand-in-hand with the surgeon to the operating suite. These events rarely, if ever, happen in reality. Sometimes what is depicted in a book may not be what actually happens in the hospital the child is entering. For example, the preparation material may say that parents will go to the surgery room with the child. One hospital in which I worked had the parents stay in the child's room while aides took the child to surgery. There are detrimental emotional effects on the child when he or she is expecting one set of reassuring circumstances and they do not happen. The net result is the possibility that all information is discounted when the child encounters a discrepancy between what was said in preparation and what actually happened to the child. Additionally, several sources of misinformation or conflicting information may lead the child to heightened anxiety, as he or she does not know what to believe or perceives that adults are trying to hide something awful from him or her.

In the area of sexual abuse prevention, concerned professionals need to be particularly cautious about the enormous spate of books, pamphlets, and audiovisual material, all purporting to make children safe from abduction. Although many of these are well-intentioned and carefully crafted presentations, others only seem to ride the wave of hysteria over missing and exploited children, rather than provide a careful analysis of the problem (Bergman, 1986). Without adequate field testing, some of these materials may overly increase children's fear of strangers, of being alone, or of being abducted and molested. On the other hand, the parent who provides such material may become satisfied the child is adequately protected and, in complacency, fail to maintain customary supervision. Thus, there are negative side effects of a bibliotherapeutic intervention (so-called iatrogenic effects).

These points relate clearly to the validity of the written materials provided to parents and children. Most books lack validation or testing of any sort to demonstrate that the books do what they purport to do. This is not a problem for most children's books written for entertainment. However, when the materials are advertised as meeting psychological needs, careful examination of the content and effects is required. In the absence of empirical validation, the practitioner must use common sense and professional judgment to weed out inappropriate books. This applies to the books listed in Table 3.2, because they may not fit individual practitioners' systems. One should always read a book before recommending it to a parent or child to insure that the contents are compatible with the practitioner's therapeutic goals. Indeed, there is nothing more embarrassing (or professionally telling) than when a patient asks questions about material in a book the practitioner provided, and answers are made in ignorance of the book.

Additionally, there are many situations where bibliotherapy would be inappropriate as a sole intervention. For example, if a child is adjusting poorly to the parents' divorce, reading a book, in the absence of therapeutic support, is unlikely to be very beneficial. With the books on parenting or "how to do" some specific parenting behavior, research has shown that overview and interaction with the practitioner is usually necessary, in addition to the book. In the case of *Toilet Training in Less Than a Day* (Azrin & Foxx, 1974), supervised use of the book enhances the success of the procedure (Butler, 1976; Matson & Ollendick, 1977). Consequently, the practitioner needs to consider whether bibliotherapy needs more professional supervision than merely handing the parent or child a book to read.

Facilitating Pediatric Interventions

Following the orientation of working within the parameters of the pediatric practice, the psychologist can help the pediatrician make his or her medical treatments more effective or without adverse psychological consequences.

Ameliorating Medical Fears

Many children express considerable fear of medical procedures and personnel. When the fear becomes exaggerated, irrational, or intense enough, it becomes maladaptive and produces conflict with the child's environment (namely with parents, teachers, doctors, and nurses). Even minor forms of medical fears may be detrimental to medical treatment and the child's well-being. The remediation of children's medical anxiety often makes the pediatrician's medical treatment more effective and safer or easier to implement. There are numerous procedures that the consultant can implement.

Many commercially available books and filmstrips in wide use purport to prepare children for medical procedures or hospitalization. Some of these are inadequate and may actually do some harm to the child by raising anxiety through misinformation. Some well-controlled research, however, has developed a few competent preparations for reducing anxiety. These preparation strategies include filmed modeling, providing accurate information about what is going to happen, giving emotional support in stressful situations, and teaching coping strategies in anticipation of stressful events (Elkins & Roberts, 1983). The psychologist can investigate and adapt these types of procedures for a particular setting and practice. In this way the consulting psychologist can use psychological principles to reduce children's anxieties about medical events. This, in turn, can facilitate the pediatrician's medical intervention through a prepared and happier child, faster recovery, fewer behavior problems, and better cooperation (Elkins & Roberts, 1983; Peterson & Brownlee-Duffeck, 1984; Siegel, 1983).

Another form of preparation to ameliorate medical anxiety and pain is hypnosis, as, for example, in the case of Annette, the 6-year-old girl with leukemia who had to undergo painful bone marrow aspirations (Case 5 in chapter 1). She resisted being restrained for the procedures and became quite anxious. The pediatrician and pediatric psychologist used a technique for Annette that included hypnotic rehearsal of the bone marrow procedure with blowing during the procedure as if blowing out birthday cake candles. This technique helped Annette prepare for the traumatic medical procedures and to endure the pain, with the result that the aspirations were completed quicker and with less discomfort (Hilgard & LeBaron, 1982).

Increasing Compliance with Medical Regimens

Children's noncompliance with recommended treatment is a critical problem frequently facing pediatricians. Presumably, if medical interventions are to be effective, they need to be rigorously followed. This might appear to be less of a problem with children than with adults because children are supposedly under the control and management of their parents or adult caregivers. However, no doubt every pediatric clinic and hospital has an unwritten list of patients who are notoriously noncompliant and frustratingly make frequent appearances for medical intervention. Estimates of noncompliance often range up to 90% of patients. Many medical treatments rely upon individual behavior being repeated over a period of time for any beneficial effects to be realized. These include, for example, continual vigilance for such disorders as diabetes, which requires dietary control and insulin self-administration, and epilepsy, which requires self-medication to control seizures. Other treatments seemingly may be simple, such as taking penicillin for strep throat; nevertheless, even these produce considerable noncompliance.

The consulting psychologist may be called in more frequently for the complex and frustrating medically noncompliant patient and not the patient who occasionally forgets a treatment. For example, I was called to the adolescent endocrinology unit to "deal with" a recalcitrant young man who repeatedly manipulated his insulin so that he could miss school or disrupt his mother's dates by going into ketoacidosis and having to go to the hospital emergency room, with the end result of hospital admission. He had not been in school a full day for over a year, and his mother spent more time in the hospital than at her job. The call with the referral came close to using the words of Drotar et al. (1982): "Have we got *one* for you!" The consultation extended beyond the unit to include the school, the family physician, both parents (divorced), and the emergency room staff on how to handle his manipulative attempts. Toward the end, I pleaded with the unit to send me an easy case next time and to refer noncompliant patients earlier *before* they became so difficult to treat.

The case of Amy (Case 4 in chapter 1) illustrates the problem of a patient not following a diabetic treatment regimen (Lowe & Lutzker, 1979). Nine-year-old Amy had been repeatedly educated about proper diet, insulin injections, and urine testing, yet she frequently went into acidosis, a potentially life-threatening situation that compliance to the regimen would have avoided. The consulting psychologists set up a behavioral program consisting of self and parental monitoring of three medical responsibilities—urine testing, diet, and foot care. Compliance for these aspects of treatment was credited on a chart if she completed the tasks at the scheduled time. In the final and successful intervention, Amy earned points for completing each of her responsibilities. These points were redeemable for daily reinforcers provided by her mother and weekly reinforcers from the psychologist. During the reward intervention and later during follow-up assessment, Amy was complying 100% of the time for all three regimen components.

The pediatric psychologist can provide very useful assistance on increasing children's and their parents' compliance with medical regimens. Noncompliance is clearly a behavioral problem for which psychological intervention can be helpful. Based on research and experience, practitioners have found that regimen compliance can be enhanced by (a) clearly informing the parents and child about the rationale for a treatment, (b) fitting the regimen to the patient's daily schedule, (c) getting a commitment from parent and child that the regimen is understood and will be followed, (d) having the pediatrician and nurses express concern over completion of the regimen, (e) utilizing step-by-step protocols and checklists to monitor compliance, and (f) establishing reward procedures for children to become initially invested in compliance and setting up natural reinforcers to maintain such compliance once established. In these ways, the pediatric psychologist can positively influence pediatric practice by furthering compliance to prescribed medical regimes.

Maintaining Psychologist Availability

The psychologist as a consultant needs to be available and approachable by the pediatrician and ancillary staff as well as by the patients and their parents. Many pediatric psychologists find it useful to structure scheduled times of availability for consultations in order to guarantee access to the psychologist.

A unique model for providing psychological services in a private pediatric group practice has been established by Carolyn Schroeder. This model is exem-ongoing program of a "call in/come in" service is provided by psychological consultants to a group of pediatricians for their patients' parents. Two hours a week are scheduled for parents to call the pediatrician's office for answers by psychologists regarding developmental, psychosocial, and behavioral questions. Any problems that cannot be handled by the phone call are referred for a "come-in" appointment with the psychologist.

In general, the interventions suggested in this service are behaviorally based and utilize changes in the environment, rewards for appropriate child behavior, and punishment or ignoring of inappropriate behavior. Additionally, much of this service involves providing information so the parents can have more realistic developmental expectations. A number of sources describe this excellent model of pediatric psychology practice (Mesibov et al., 1977; Schroeder, 1979; Schroeder, Goolsby, & Stangler, 1975; Schroeder, Gordon, Kanoy, & Routh, 1983). A recent evaluation of the service over a period of time found that short-term interventions could be provided successfully through this pediatric primary-care setting (Kanoy & Schroeder, 1985). Parents rated the service and the telephone counselors as valuable. Thus, the call in/come in service can be a cost-effective way of maintaining the psychologist's availability to parents.

A similar telephone consultation service for parents called "Parentline" has been set up through a university-based clinic to answer parents' questions about problems in development, behavior, and learning (Newcomb, Chenkin, Card, & Ialongo, 1984). In a similar pediatric consultation program, the pediatrician faced with psychological questions about behavior or child management refers the parents to a psychologist who maintains scheduled hours at the pediatrician's office (Morgan & Cullen, 1980). The service has been well-received by parents and the referring pediatricians because of its timeliness for making effective behavioral interventions. The pediatric psychologist can adapt these programs to meet particular needs of the medical setting for access and availability of the consultant.

Developing Consultation Liaisons

A consultation service oriented to pediatric *practice* can be an exciting development, with multiple roles to be created. This approach can result in numerous advantages to the psychologist and pediatrician and to the patients and their families. There are, however, some important considerations before attempting to put a consultation into actual practice.

In developing a consultative relationship, the psychologist is advised to start cautiously in taking cases or providing psychological assistance. As in all work, the psychologist should be wary of overpromising results that may not be deliverable given the difficulty of many cases presenting in the pediatric setting. The fledgling pediatric psychologist might start with a few cases and, after gaining some success where results can be demonstrated, gradually expand to a fuller caseload. Ottinger and Roberts (1980) describe how a pediatric psychology clinical service started with an offering of consultation for a few cases in circumscribed areas rather than overwhelming the pediatrician in a "gangbuster" style of "we can cure all your problems." The proposal to provide psychological services was prefaced by the statement that the psychologists thought they had something worthwhile to offer; the physician could try the service, and, if it fulfilled a need, then greater involvement might be considered. If a need was not met, or if the physician saw the service as incompetent or inappropriate, no further referrals would be made to the service. All personnel associated with the pediatric psychology service attempted to provide competent, immediate action on each referral and to inform the pediatrician of action and progress through notes and telephone calls. Similarly, the pediatrician committed to informing the service about the initial and ongoing medical aspects of each case. Although a written contract was not formalized, there was clear agreement on the roles and functions of everybody in the service.

The pediatrician is not likely to hand over "lock and key" to his or her practice and patients, even to the greatest pediatric psychologist. Thus, the consultant needs to be alert to the proprietary element of medical practice and to be sensitive to such turf issues when they might arise. This can be ameliorated somewhat by providing feedback to the pediatrician regarding what has been done and why, as well as when and why interventions were successful or unsuccessful. This feedback will promote realistic expectations by the physician and perhaps increase more appropriate referrals.

Communication with the pediatrician and allied personnel (social workers, nurses, child life workers) is essential to building a consultation liaison service. Of course, as in all activities, pediatric psychologists will need to rely on their social skills in negotiating and carrying on consultantships. Although pediatricians have been found to be most open to collaboration, the pediatrician, in many respects, is a consumer, and the psychologist is a salesperson marketing a service.

Before starting to develop a psychological consultation service in a hospital or on an outpatient basis, the pediatric psychologist may find it useful to review how other such services developed. For example, Koocher, Sourkes, and Keane (1979) describe how their pediatric psychological consultation on a pediatric oncology division expanded from ad hoc crisis intervention on an intermittent basis to an integrated system providing "consistent and routinely scheduled consultation." A gradual development of increasing involvement occurred over time: initiating daily ward visits (rounds), holding team meetings with other staff, providing direct therapeutic contact with patients and families, providing in-service training with other staff, and playing larger roles in patient case management.

Similarly, Drotar et al. (1982) outline the growth of pediatric psychology in a large multispecialty hospital where both teaching and case-oriented strategies were utilized in working with pediatric personnel. Their activities included weekly psychosocial rounds and meetings on several inpatient divisions (the units for infant/toddlers, young school-age children who are chronically ill or terminally ill, and orthopedics), as well as individual case consultation. These and other descriptions of consultation services (Brewer, 1978; Geist, 1977; Lewis, 1978; Roberts, Quevillon, & Wright, 1979; Walker, 1979a; Wright, 1979a) can assist in identifying approaches to becoming successful consultants and in avoiding pitfalls sometimes encountered when working with other health-care personnel.

Issues in Consultation

Despite the opportunities for consultation, there are, at times, interfering issues that arise. Recognition of these issues can aid the development of successful consultant relationships. These issues include concerns over whose turf the psychologist is working on, differences in professional language and concepts, misperceptions of roles of psychologists, differences between practice in medical centers and in private clinics, and too many inappropriate referrals. Although it is glib to assert that pediatric psychology consultation will grow as long as competent services are provided (Roberts et al., 1982), these issues of difficulty in consultation transcend even competence and professionalism.

Turf Issues

The psychologist should, of course, recognize where one is and with whom one is working. When a psychologist works in a medical setting, he or she enters a culture somewhat alien to a psychological background. Furthermore, a slightly different set of values is notable within a definite hierarchy of power and relationships. The psychologist may interact professionally with physicians, but actually more intensively sometimes with nurses and such allied health staff as occupational therapists, child-life workers, social workers, among others. Some knowledge of the training and philosophical orientations of these disciplines will be useful in valuing each one's contributions and understanding how and why they might act in certain ways.

In medical settings, the physician remains at the top of the power structure and usually controls most referrals and practice opportunities for the pediatric psychologist (Drotar, 1982). For this reason, considerable attention is given in chapter 2 and the current chapter to pediatric training and practice orientations with implications for psychologists. Despite the name changes of many medical centers to "health centers," there have not been corresponding changes in the power structures of physicians vis-à-vis other health professionals. When developing consultant relationships, I have found it prudent to inquire of a referring physician about how he or she wants to work together on the case. Does the physician want an evaluation and report before any psychological treatment is commenced? How does the physician want feedback? Does the physician want to see the child and family conjointly with the psychologist? In this way, the relationship and expectations for both professionals are more clearly articulated in advance. The psychologist need not relinquish his or her own authority or responsibility, but the answer to the question "Whose patient is this?" can be determined early and usually to the satisfaction of both parties.

Once, as I tried to implement a standard tracheotomy addiction treatment procedure with a child (e.g., Wright et al., 1968, 1969), a medical resident in otorhynolaryngology (ear, nose, and throat), who also had been called to consult by the neonatologist in the intensive care nursery, repeatedly wrote medical orders overriding the psychological protocol to which the interdisciplinary team had agreed. I still recall vividly the gut-wrenching agony and anger I had as I argued with the resident over treatment procedures. This predicament might have been avoided had I clarified in advance with the neonatologist about "Whose patient is this?" in a more diplomatic way then the subvocal question seems to imply.

Language Differences

All disciplines employ jargon as shorthand expressions or language peculiar to each profession. When disciplines interact, the jargon frequently impedes communication. Psychologists are as guilty of this as others; it is just that we understand ourselves more than we do them. Knowledge of commonly used phrases, jargon, and abbreviations is helpful to the psychologist entering the medical arena. Although asking what something means is usually a good way to learn, this approach can be threatening to the professional facade of competence we often erect in a consultation. Some basic abbreviations are listed in Table 3.3, but there are considerably more. Some of the major pediatric medical texts provide discussions of these abbreviations and the processes they signify (see chapter 5). Unfortunately, some texts merely perpetuate the mystery of the acronyms and jargon.

Conceptualization Differences

Physicians and psychologists, by virtue of their respective training, often approach problems differently. Case conceptualizations relate to how patients' problems are thought about. Physicians use a process of "differential diagnosis," which is a logical procedure of considering a number of possible causes for a medical symptom and then systematically "ruling out" competing hypotheses until a conclusion is empirically and logically derived. Although psychology uses the term differential diagnosis, it is rare that systematic assessment is undertaken with the same underlying conceptualization as in medicine. Psychologists tend to use diagnostic testing to "rule in" a preconceived diagnosis. However, case conceptualization in the medical approach clearly resembles the scientific approach of psychology that too often is divorced from clinical work—observation and

Table 3.3. Medical Terms and Abbreviations

bid	twice a day (to take medicine)	IM	intramuscular injection
BRP	bathroom privileges	IV	intravenous
BUN	blood urea nitrogen test	LAF	Laminar Flow Room (a sterile
BM	bowel movement		protected hospital room)
BP	blood pressure	LP	lumbar puncture
Ca	carcinoma	MMR	immunization for measles,
CA	cancer		mumps, and rubella
CBC	complete blood count	NPO	nothing by mouth, usually no
CC	chief complaint		food or water
CHD	congenital heart disease	otitis media	ear infection
c/o	complains of	PE or Px	physical examination
cv	cardiovascular	PO	by mouth
decub	lying down	PKU	phenylketonuria
DOB	date of birth	pr	per rectum
DPT	immunization for diptheria,	PRN	as needed, whenever necessary
	pertussis, and tetanus	prog	prognosis
Dx	diagnosis	q	every or each
emesis	vomiting	qd	every day
ENT	ear, nose, throat specialist or	RBC	red blood count
	medical department; also could	R/O	rule out
	be listed as ORL for	Rx	treatment, prescription
	otorhynolaryngology	SSE	soap suds enema
Fleets	brand-name enema	stat	immediately
FUO	fever of unknown origin	syncope	fainting
Fx	fracture	TCDB	turn, cough, and deep breathe
gavage	feeding through tube into	tid	three times a day
	stomach through nose	U/A	urinalysis
GI	gastrointestinal	UCD	usual childhood diseases
GU	genitourinary	URI	upper respiratory infection
HA	headache	UTI	urinary tract infection
hem-onc	hematology-oncology specialist	VS	vital signs
Hgb	hemoglobin		
I & O	intake and output		
	(e.g., of fluids)		

generation of hypotheses and alternatives, testing of hypotheses through experimental procedures, analysis of results, and establishing conclusions based on empirical results.

Pediatricians may use one of several organizational frameworks for conceptualizing cases (Morgan & Engel, 1969). For example, in medical centers, case write-ups may include sections on a child's birth history, nutritional history, immunization record, growth and developmental history, and physical examination findings. SOAP is the acronym for another framework for progress notes wherein each letter denotes a section: Subjective data—gathered from the patient; Objective data—from physical examination and laboratory tests; Assessment—interpretation of data and results; Plan—diagnostic impressions, treatment interventions, patient or family education, and follow-up. A third framework, the Problem-Oriented Medical Record, is a more detailed, comprehensive organization for presenting data (Nelson et al., 1975). The POMR organization is logically structured and is frequently used in teaching hospitals, but it requires considerable paperwork. The pediatric psychologist can gain a basic understanding of pediatric diagnosis in a practical manual by Athreya (1980).

At the crux of medical diagnosis is the "ruling-out" process. For example, the case conceptualization for Karen's complaints of stomach pain (Case 2 in chapter 1) first required ruling out physical causes for the pains before the pediatrician could reach the diagnosis that the problem was maintained by environmental contingencies, that is, a psychological problem (Miller & Kratochwill, 1979). In the case of Oscar's failure to thrive (Case 1), the attending physicians needed to rule out several potential physical causes, including a malabsorption problem, organic pathology, and seizure disorder (Roberts & Horner, 1979). With Joey's encopresis (Case 3), the physician had to rule out the possibility of a physical abnormality causing the fecal retention, such as Hirschsprung's disease or spinal cord injury (Roberts et al., 1977; see also Wright & Walker, 1977). This ruling out of physical causes is necessary because, in all three cases, a pediatric psychological intervention would have had little impact had the problems been totally physical. Indeed, behavioral interventions for the physical problems that were ruled out would have likely exacerbated the problems.

Medical Center or Private Practice Pediatricians

Most aspects of consultation in pediatric psychology relate equally to any type of medical setting. Some differences are apparent, such as fewer ancillary resources in private practice than in large medical centers, but the commonalities are large. An awareness of where the pediatrician is practicing is important, however. The American Medical Association lists 23,516 physicians who have designated themselves as pediatricians (American Medical Association, 1976, 1977); of these, 21,092 are classified in the direct patient-care category. Correspondingly, the American Academy of Pediatrics comprises 14,429 Fellows, with only 23% of these in academic medicine, that is, medical schools or teaching institutions (Burnett & Bell, 1978). Thus, the vast majority of pediatricians are engaged in office practice, either singly or in a group. In contrast, much of the professional focus of pediatric psychology has derived from the teaching hospital setting, where more pediatric psychologists are to be found. Yet, most of the pediatricians and their patients are not found in large medical centers.

Drotar et al. (1982) described pediatric psychology consultation in a large hospital-based practice, and Roberts and Wright (1982) have outlined outpatient practice approaches. The outpatient or private pediatric practice is an area for considerable expansion of pediatric psychology, given the large numbers of pediatricians in practice and the patients seen (Kanoy & Schroeder, 1985; Schroeder, 1979). Practice in the medical center, however, offers some unique challenges, given the frequently more severe problems encountered and the opportunities for interdisciplinary work.

Types of Referrals

Table 2.1 in chapter 2 depicted the range of problems referred to three pediatric psychology services. It should be remembered, however, that these were fairly well-developed units. In many cases, pediatricians and other physicians do not have a clear idea of what a psychologist does or can contribute. The perception of psychologists as "testers" sometimes prevails (Drotar et al., 1982). This limited perception frequently leads to requests for testing, with only vague notions of why the physician wants it done or what the evaluation will provide. However, if these opportunities for consultation are handled with professional diplomacy and the idea of educating the physician, a strong consultative relationship can be built. Sometimes the vague referral for an IQ test is simply a request for help on a troubling case.

Generally, in establishing consultantships, a gradual process of establishing credibility and encouraging more appropriate referrals takes place. Pediatric psychologists have noted that some initial referrals are "tests" of competence by the physician. As noted earlier in this chapter, Drotar et al. (1982) recall doctors prefacing their referrals to the consultation–liaison service with "Have I got one for you!" (p. 240). These referrals are often the most difficult cases a service encounters, such as the notoriously noncompliant diabetic adolescent in the endocrinology clinic or the hallucinating and paranoid burn patient. These are part of pediatric psychology and, of course, must be faced, and, it is hoped, successfully resolved.

Drotar et al. (1982) suggest: "Interested questions, data gathering, supportive empathizing with the physician's predicament, and specifying what psychological consultation can realistically provide are techniques that can gradually help shape mutually adaptive professional roles and foster good working relationships" (p. 240). Basically, being available and appropriately educating medical personnel about psychology's potential contributions will expand opportunities for consultation. Nevertheless, the psychologist can often earn a pediatrician's gratitude by relieving him or her of a particularly burdensome case. However, psychologists who get cases "dumped" on them may find themselves with cases they, in turn, find irremediable. One would not want a psychological consultantship consisting entirely of troublesome, complex cases with little reward; expansion into other roles would be more exciting and probably more beneficial to more patients in the long run.

Chapter 4

Pediatric Psychology Practices

The practice of pediatric psychology offers a mixture of cases from the frequently seen to the novel. Yet, depending on the particular practice setting and the psychologist's own interests, the usual case for one may be the unusual in another situation. The range of problems is exemplified by the six cases in chapter 1 and by the case problems listed in Table 2.1 in chapter 2.

For the psychologist consulting to an oncology unit, for example, practice may involve preparing children for bone marrow aspiration, diminishing anticipatory effects of chemotherapy, helping a child adapt to physical changes (e.g., hair loss) associated with radiation therapy, counseling school teachers on easing the re-entry of a leukemic child into the classroom, and providing support to families, especially siblings, during critical periods and in the event of death. Similar activities might be performed by the psychologist consulting for other chronic diseases such as cystic fibrosis, asthma, and physical handicaps.

In contrast, the psychologist on the neonate and toddler units might be faced with a day's activities of assessing the feeding habits of a failure-to-thrive infant and its mother, evaluating the developmental status of a hospitalized baby, consulting on infant stimulation interventions with an occupational therapist and on home-care resources with a social worker, implementing a procedure for weaning a child off its breathing dependency on a tracheotomy tube, meeting with an interdisciplinary treatment team on cases in a premature infant nursery, and explaining the psychological implications of prematurity to new parents.

Outpatient practice similarly requires a versatility of skills. For example, a day's cases may include training for the parents of a behaviorally noncompliant, but medically healthy, 9-year-old child, counseling a diabetic adolescent who is noncompliant with treatment regimens, consulting with parents of a 2-year-old about toilet training, setting up a dry-bed procedure for an enuretic 7-year-old child, conducting a developmental evaluation of a child slow to grow and talk, assessing a child considered for enrichment classes, counseling an anorexic adolescent, and consulting a school about a child complaining of recurrent stomach pains. Other outpatient work may include providing therapy for a sexually abused child, implementing a sexual abuse prevention program in the schools, consulting to a community hospital on preparing children for hospitalization and surgery, or devising community-wide incentive programs to increase children's use of safety belts.

All of the settings and activities discussed here involve much the same psychological tools required in other more traditional clinical child practices. However, the key differences are sometimes the setting, but, more importantly, the types of cases seen. Pediatric psychology practice involves assessment, intervention, follow-up, and prevention for a wide array of medical and psychological problems. This chapter will describe the various areas of pediatric psychological practice.

Assessment and prevention are two of the areas that are basic psychological activities; the remaining five areas constitute the problems and types of disorders comprising pediatric psychology work (acute physical disorders, chronic physical disorders, psychosomatic disorders, and developmental disorders). Assessment and intervention will be described in each of these areas.

ASSESSMENT

Proper assessment of problems lays the groundwork for decision making about the course of psychological interventions. As in all psychological practices, the pediatric psychologist must carefully evaluate the patient, his or her family, the problem, and the circumstances. Pediatric psychological assessment has as its purpose to aid in the development of an intervention or treatment for the patient and family. Assessment and intervention are, by necessity, interwoven. Some traditional practices have directed assessment toward diagnostic labeling or categorization, with little focus on differential diagnosis as conceptualized in chapter 3, with minimal input on differential selection of intervention, and with no ability to evaluate the outcome of a therapeutic strategy (Roberts & La Greca, 1981). However, the intensive and busy nature of pediatric psychology practice does not permit nonproductive assessments. Additionally, the developmental perspective noted in chapter 2 conveys the need to assess within a developmental framework (Magrab, 1984a; Roberts, Maddux, & Wright, 1984). For example, Magrab's framework for assessment includes cognitive, language, motor, and social development of the child who may be ill or handicapped.

Magrab's (1984b) volume is an excellent source on psychological and behavioral assessment in pediatric psychology. Karoly and May's (in press) book also describes assessment in child-health psychology. Other child-assessment texts are sometimes useful, but are less focused on pediatric problems (e.g., Mash &

Terdal, 1981; Weaver, 1984). The pragmatic orientation of pediatric psychologists, also noted in chapter 2, requires that assessment tools be selected carefully depending on the specific problem.

Rarely will a standardized battery of tests produce useful and necessary information to devise effective treatment strategies. For example, some clinical child psychologists routinely administer a test battery, perhaps consisting of the Wechsler Intelligence Scale for Children-Revised (WISC-R), the Children's Apperception Test, a drawing test, one or another achievement tests, e.g., Wide Range Achievement Test-Revised or Peabody Individual Achievement Test (WRAT-R or PIAT) and a Personality Inventory for Children or a problem behavior checklist. Although such testing generates considerable data, not all of it is necessary for every case, even in traditional clinical child practices. Thus, psychologists need to develop some diagnostic test restraint, assessing only what is actually needed. Additionally, such a standardized battery would have limited utility in a pediatric psychology practice receiving referrals of medical noncompliance, failure to thrive, adjustment to burns, and terminal illness.

Pediatric psychologists sometimes use global projective and objective assessment techniques, yet these practices follow more traditional approaches of clinical child psychology. For these, further information can be gained in generic and specialized child assessment texts (see chapter 5). More targeted assessment tools are required to answer questions posed by the pediatric psychologist practitioner and the case circumstances. There are several assessment approaches adapted to pediatric psychology work, including developmental assessment, interviewing, and behavioral assessment.

Developmental Assessment

Evaluation of development involves determining whether a child is functioning at an appropriate level for his or her age and if future development is predicted to be normal or abnormal (Lichtenstein & Ireton, 1984; Wright et al., 1979). Developmental assessment typically deals with infants and toddlers, whereas intelligence testing involves older children. The tendency is to consider developmental indices as equivalent to intelligence test scores. This practice is unfortunate and erroneous.

Although several assessment instruments are now available, the Bayley Scales of Infant Development (Bayley, 1969) have generally received the widest acceptance as a well standardized, valid, and reliable measure of development. The Bayley consists of three sections producing three developmental indices: Motor Development (called the PDI for Psychomotor Development Index), Mental Development Index (MDI), and Infant Behavior Record. The PDI assesses motor functioning, such as crawling and object manipulation, and the MDI measures sensorimotor functioning. The Infant Behavior Record is used to record behaviors observed during the test's administration. The Bayley test provides standardized situations in which to measure whether a child exhibits an age-appropriate response (imitating scribbling, putting pegs in a board, picking up plastic cubes). Pediatric psychologists often use the Bayley to assess the present, overall developmental status of a child and to identify areas of delayed development that require stimulation and intervention.

Many pediatricians and nurses rely upon the Denver Developmental Screening Test (DDST: Frankenburg et al., 1981) to screen for developmental delays in their pediatric patients. This practice is appropriate when the DDST is limited to the screening function, with more intensive assessment done by the psychologist with the Bayley for cases indicating problems. Another pediatric approach to measuring infants' abilities is the Neonatal Behavioral Assessment Scale (usually called by the name of its developer, Brazelton, a pediatrician; Als, Lester, Tronick, & Brazelton, 1982; Brazelton, 1984). Some pediatricians and psychologists also use the Minnesota Child Development Inventory (MCDI) to screen the development of children ages 1 to 6 years based on parental report (Gottfried, Guerin, Spencer, & Meyer, 1984; Ireton & Thwing, 1974). Several other infant and child development scales are available (see Magrab, 1984b; Wright et al., 1979).

Developmental assessment is frequently necessary for the medical–psychological condition of failure to thrive, in which infants do not grow with no physical cause apparent (as, for example, in the case of Oscar, Case 1 in chapter 1). As described later in the present chapter, psychological assessment of Oscar with the Bayley scales determined that developmental delays were present in his motor and psychological functioning and indicated where the treatment team should make targeted interventions. In Oscar's case, as with many infant cases, repeated assessment with the Bayley scales also helped demonstrate changes and progress due to the various medical and psychological interventions.

Interviewing

Interviewing is a well-accepted method for gathering information in psychological and pediatric practices. In almost all situations, interviews with parents, the child patient, relatives, and teachers can provide useful data for conceptualizing the problem. Structured interviews have been increasing in use, with particular attention to applications in pediatric settings. For example, Webb and Van Devere (1985) have developed an interview format for assessing pediatric patients' verbalized affective distress. The Structured Pediatric Psychosocial Interview (SPPI) involves 200 items for the school-age and adolescent child. Several investigations in a pediatric psychology and psychiatry practice indicate that children can reveal clinically useful information via the SPPI on their perceptions of psychosocial stresses. There are four major scales measuring the pediatric patient's concerns in terms of distress in Thinking, Relating, Feeling, and Impetuosity. The SPPI asks such questions as: "How do people know when you are angry?" "What sorts of things make you happy?" Scoring is based on the child's answers. Technical coding and scale interpretation then aid in using the SPPI data for decision making and understanding a child's developmental psychopathology.

The Child Assessment Schedule (CAS) is another structured interview that also has received research attention for its applicability in pediatric settings (Hodges, Kline, Fitch, McKnew, & Cytryn, 1981; Hodges, Kline, Stern, Cytryn, & McKnew, 1982). The CAS takes about 45 minutes to administer and consists of two parts, including 75 questions for the child and 53 items based on the examiner's observations. The questions are incorporated in a fairly informal discussion covering such areas as activities, fears, self-image, somatic concerns, and mood. The examiner's observations include such areas as insight, grooming, estimates of cognitive ability, and quality of emotional expression. The data gathered in the CAS are combined to determine a diagnosis from the *Diagnostic and Statistical Manual of Mental Disorders* (DSM-III, American Psychiatric Association, 1980) and to implement treatments. Preliminary reports indicate that the CAS is valid and reliable. However, despite the clinical utility of both the SPPI and CAS, these are not in widespread use in pediatric psychology practice. Many more pediatric psychologists rely on less structured means of gathering information, perhaps to the neglect of comprehensive assessment.

As a guide to interviews with children and parents, practitioners frequently use the A–B–C model of behavioral assessment (Mash & Terdal, 1981; Roberts & La Greca, 1981; Robinson & Eyberg, 1984). Each letter in the model signifies a key component in the interview. The A represents the antecedents, B, the problematic behavior, and C, the consequences of the behavior. Although, conceptually, the behavioral model holds that behavior is learned, with antecedent and consequent events integral in the acquisition and maintenance of behavior, the pediatric psychologist need not embrace this behavioral conceptualization in order to find the A–B–C guide useful.

The A–B–C model produces a more complete idea of what the problem is within the situation. For the Behavior, interviewers often ask for clarification, such as "What do you mean?" or "With whom, how often, and where does it occur?" (Roberts & La Greca, 1981). For Antecedents, the pediatric psychologist might ask, "When does the behavior occur and in what situations or contexts?" For example, psychosocial antecedents for the behavior of stomach pain complaints might be Monday mornings before school, after returning from a visitation with a noncustodial parent, or a request from a parent to clean up a room. Consequence events are those that follow the behavior and might include the actions of other persons such as inadvertent rewarding, that might influence a behavior. In the case of stomachaches, the child might get to stay home from school, which would increase the likelihood of recurrence (e.g., as in the case of Amy, Case 4 in chapter 1). This elementary framework of A–B–C for interviewing often provides sufficient detail to implement interventions or to guide more detailed assessment, including observations, checklists, or other tools.

Observations

Practitioners conduct direct observations of children, families, and pediatric staff to understand a presenting problem. In pediatric work, a psychologist may observe such situations as the eating behavior of a pediatric inpatient child to assess the rate and manner of intake relative to failure to thrive (Roberts & Horner, 1979) or the interactions between a parent and a child relative to a noncompliance behavior problem (Forehand & McMahon, 1981). Pediatric psychologists also observe children in structured situations to determine activity level (Routh & Schroeder, 1976; Routh, Schroeder, & O'Tuama, 1974) or to understand mouthing and pica behavior of children hospitalized for lead poisoning (Madden, Russo, & Cataldo, 1980a, 1980b). Alternatively, coded observations may be useful for determining children's anxiety in arousing situations, perhaps requiring psychological intervention to remediate (e.g., Glennon & Weisz, 1978; Jay, Ozolins, Elliott, & Caldwell, 1983), and for assessing children's activity levels in naturalistic settings such as a classroom (Abikoff, Gittleman-Klein, & Klein, 1977). Other pediatric psychology observations have been conducted in homes of children with cystic fibrosis to determine family interaction and adjustment (Kucia et al., 1979) or in hospital wards for measuring child and staff behaviors in a pediatric intensive care unit (Cataldo, Bessman, Parker, Pearson, & Rogers, 1979).

Observations provide the pediatric psychologist with information about the behavior of interest in addition to antecedents and consequences. A clearer understanding of the situation can usually be gained through observations. Hospital-based practice of pediatric psychology often permits more direct observation than outpatient work where structured and analog situations can be used in addition to home and school visits. There is an extensive literature on child observation strategies, with attention to its problems of reactivity, reliability, validity, observer bias, and drift (Mash & Terdal, 1981; Roberts & La Greca, 1981).

Observations are most often done informally, without consideration of these limitations, because they can be used profitably in a variety of settings and with numerous patient populations and problem behaviors. Pediatric psychologists have used considerable ingenuity in observations to enhance their understanding and improve interventions.

Chapter 5 lists references for the pediatric psychology practitioner to consult on general assessment issues and on evaluating specific disorders such as pain, anorexia nervosa, depression, and other problems. The state of assessment in pediatric psychology parallels the state of assessment in general psychological practice: Whereas some techniques show merit and promise, there remains a great need for development and refinement of diagnostic tools leading to effective intervention

(Russo, Bird, & Masek, 1980). Again, pediatric psychology calls up the creativity of the practitioner.

ACUTE PHYSICAL DISORDERS

There are a number of physical disorders for which medical treatments have had limited success, but that are amenable to psychological intervention. These disorders may have entirely physical bases for which psychological treatments are, nevertheless, useful. Alternatively, the disorder may have physical symptoms resulting from psychological factors, for which psychological intervention also is necessary. Disorders can be categorized on a number of continua—the typical dichotomy is acute (relatively short-term) versus chronic (long-term or lifelong). The next section describes pediatric psychological activities related to chronic physical disorders.

Acute physical disorders include such problems as otitis media (ear infections), gastrointestinal and respiratory infections, and usual childhood diseases (UCD in medical jargon; e.g., chicken pox), although some diseases are much less prevalent today due to immunization (e.g., mumps, measles, polio, whooping cough). Some acute physical disorders have more psychological implications than others. For example, accumulating evidence indicates that recurrent otitis media may have serious concomitants, such as poor language and reading development, and impaired social functioning (Gottlieb, 1983). Primary deficits of perceptual–motor skills and abstract thinking ability are the more debilitating sequelae to the acute condition of meningitis brought on by hemophilus influenza (Wright & Jimmerson, 1971). As these disorders illustrate, pediatric disorders of immediate medical concern, which have effective physical treatments, can have long-lasting psychological effects. Psychological assessment and intervention with such cases can often prevent or ameliorate adverse sequelae.

Burns

Childhood burns pose an immediate medical concern and also raise psychological considerations. Despite the fact that most burn situations are preventable (Wright et al., 1979), burns are one of the most frequent injuries among children. Severe childhood burns are particularly traumatic for their physical, social, and psychological effects. In addition to the initial burn trauma, medical treatment can be prolonged and painful. Disfigurement and complications contribute further to the psychological trauma. Many children express considerable psychological distress following a burn and during medical treatments such as debridement (removal of dead skin), dressing changes, medication for infection, and skin grafts. The many psychological aspects of burns are well-reviewed by Wisely, Masur, and Morgan (1983). Pain particularly becomes a focal point for the patient, and can be the point for psychological intervention.

The case of Amy (Case 6 in chapter 1) illustrates a multimethod approach to the multiple problems associated with burns (Walker & Healy, 1980). Amy had been burned over 80% of her body. During her hospitalization, she became fearful of and resisted the medical treatments, refused to eat, and resisted physiotherapy. Specifically, she displayed an extreme fear of dressing changes, which generalized to all interactions with medical staff. The pediatric psychologists used behavioral techniques to reduce her anxiety. These included relaxation training and emotive imagery for eliciting positive emotional responses during dressing changes under the guidance of the psychologist. A behavioral contract was negotiated for sessions when Amy exhibited cooperative behavior; she earned letter grades exchangeable for game playing or book reading with the therapist. Amy became more cooperative, resulting in shorter dressing sessions. More positive interactions with staff were enhanced. Another intervention was aimed at increasing her eating, a critical necessity given the increased needs for caloric intake during treatment. She was initially resistant, but when given control over monitoring her eating behavior, Amy was able to keep up a necessary level of calories.

Other aspects of psychological treatment included bibliotherapy, mutual story telling, and play therapy. Parent counseling was provided to address their feelings of fear, guilt, and anger, and to restore their feelings of parental adequacy. Counseling also helped to facilitate family acceptance of Amy. The mother became a social reinforcement for Amy's exercising as part of physical therapy. This multimodal treatment of the psychological concomitants of a severe burn demonstrates the facility of a variety of therapies that are sometimes necessary for pediatric psychologists. Other such cases of psychological intervention in the rehabilitation of burned children are available (e.g., Kelley, Jarvie, Middlebrook, McNeer, & Drabman, 1984; St. Lawrence & Drabman, 1983).

Encopresis

Other acute conditions are amenable to psychological interventions in order to treat the basic medical problem. A prime example of this is the problem of encopresis noted earlier. Fecal incontinence has been a frequent and difficult problem faced by parents and pediatricians. There are variations in the specifics of the presenting problem itself that interfere with definitive conceptualization. Increasingly, however, recognition is growing in children's health care that encopresis is most profitably considered a pediatric psychological problem requiring conjoint interventions.

The *DSM-III* includes the following criteria for encopresis: (a) repeated voluntary and involuntary movement of feces in inappropriate places, (b) at least one inappropriate passage of feces per month after 4 years of age, and (c) physical disorders must be ruled out (e.g., aganglionic megacolon or Hirschsprung's disease). There have been several nosologies for categorizing varieties of encopresis. Of these, the most useful for psychologists appears to be that of Walker (1978),

who presents three broad categories of encopresis based on his review of the literature. His framework includes manipulative soiling, chronic diarrhea, or irritable
bowel syndrome (often a reaction to chronic stress or anxiety), and chronic constipation with impaction, megacolon, and diarrhea-like seepage of feces around
the impaction. The last category appears to comprise the majority of encopretic
cases. Despite the intuitive appeal and clinical support for the notion of tailoring
different treatment methods for specific subtypes of encopresis, there has been,
thus far, no research showing that such differential diagnosis leads to either differential treatments or differential prognosis.

There are several physiological factors producing symptoms similar to encopresis, including dietary factors, allergies to certain foods, hypothyroidism, lead poisoning, and intestinal diseases and malformations. In all cases of childhood
encopresis symptoms, the possible involvement of organic factors should be vigor-
ously evaluated before functional or psychological factors are considered. Once
all possible organic causes for encopretic-like symptoms have been ruled out,
there are a number of treatment procedures that some pediatricians turn to first:
enemas, suppositories, drugs, anal dilation, and mineral oil. These are often not
effective in a majority of cases. Thus, more intensive interventions may be necessary, involving specialized treatment of the psychological bases of the encopresis.
The pediatric psychologist frequently gets referrals of these cases.

A number of behavior modification techniques have been developed for treating
encopresis using operant conditioning. These include contingent positive reinforcement (rewards) to increase the frequency of appropriate defecation, the withholding of such reinforcement when soiling occurs, and, in some cases, other
forms of punishment for soiling.

The basic procedures for using reward techniques were developed and
described by Logan Wright (1973, 1975). His approach is not strictly a reinforcement model, because it combines medical procedures with extensive use of
rewards. In his approach, under a physician's overview, an enema is used first to
thoroughly evacuate the child's colon. A behavior contract between parent and
child is arranged, formally establishing expectations regarding acceptable toileting and the criteria for earning rewards. Then, upon rising each morning, the
child goes to the bathroom to attempt a bowel movement voluntarily. If the child is
able to defecate a quantity of feces (e.g., 1/4 to 1/2 cup), then the parent gives the
child a small reward (e.g., money, toy, candy). If the child does not have a bowel
movement, no reward is given at that point, and the parent instead inserts a glyc-
erin suppository to assist the child in defecating. In the meantime, the child eats
breakfast and then attempts to defecate again. If he or she is successful, a smaller
reward is provided. If the child is unsuccessful, an enema is given and no reward
is given. Should the child soil during the day, a mild punishment may be employed
(e.g., no TV, sit in a chair for 10 to 15 minutes).

This entire procedure focuses on inducing the child to defecate regularly, so that
a habit is established, tone is returned to the colon, and a high probability behav-

ior is provided for the parents to reward and thereby strengthen. The reward is considered the most essential component to this program. As noted, rewards may be tangible items such as coins, lollipops, or small toys, or may be symbolic tokens (e.g., gummed stars, poker chips) that may be traded in for "back-up" reinforcers such as extra TV time, free playtime with parents, or favored recreational activities. All rewards and punishments, as well as the use of physical assistance, are gradually weaned out over time. Wright and Walker (1977) have reported a success rate of nearly 100% in their use of this approach with more than 100 cases.

The case of Joey (Case 3 in chapter 1) illustrates the problem of encopresis and its pediatric psychological treatment (Roberts et al., 1977). Joey was a 4-year-old boy who was retaining feces for lengthy periods ranging from several days to a week at a time for over 18 months. He was soiling and occasionally passing whole movements into his clothing. He entered the hospital for x-ray studies to rule out bowel abnormalities. A behavioral training program was instituted wherein he was told that whenever he used the toilet, he would immediately receive a lollipop and his mother's praise. Earning the lollipop also meant that Joey could spend 30 minutes of play with his parents doing whatever he desired after dinner. When he accidentally defected in his clothing, he was changed without comment and was told he should have used the toilet. He did not get a lollipop or the play period. Approximately 1 1/2 weeks after setting up the program, Joey started using the toilet appropriately and continued having daily bowel movements. The lollipop was phased out gradually through a renegotiation of the "contract" to a lollipop every other time, every third time, and so on until it was no longer needed.

Feeding Disorders

The treatment detail provided here illustrates pediatric psychological interventions for encopresis as an acute physical disorder. Additional medical problems with psychological treatments include a variety of feeding disturbances such as food refusal, pica, rumination, and psychogenic vomiting. Feeding disturbances occur frequently, either as a primary problem or as a corollary to other disorders such as failure to thrive or mental retardation.

Linscheid (1978, 1983) comprehensively reviewed the literature on eating disorders from a pediatric psychology perspective. Pica refers to a child (or even an adult) habitually ingesting inedible substances such as paint, plaster, and clay. Pica is a particular problem when the substances contain lead with the potential for lead poisoning and subsequent mental retardation or neurological impairments. Madden et al. (1980a, 1980b) studied pica in children and successfully intervened with children who were lead poisoned. Behavioral strategies included (a) discrimination training, (b) correspondence training and reinforcement for nonpica behaviors, and (c) differential reinforcement of other behaviors and overcorrection.

Children's food refusal, as another feeding disturbance, can lead to severe effects with long-term implications for development of anorexia nervosa. With young children, food refusal often takes the form of resisting solid foods as the child moves from breast milk to bottle formula. In the case of Oscar (Case 1 in chapter 1), food refusal was related to his failure-to-thrive condition (Roberts & Horner, 1979). Oscar refused certain foods by spitting up, closing his mouth, and turning his head when offered a spoonful. For example, he would refuse cereals and egg yolk, but accept fruit. A behavioral program was initiated whereby Oscar had to eat a spoonful of less preferred food (e.g., eggs) before being given a spoonful of the food he liked (e.g., fruit). The number of spoons of less preferred food was gradually increased before he received fruit.

A second observation made in the behavior analysis of feeding was that Oscar took longer than the usual amount of time for meals. His mother was observed to offer spoons of food at a more rapid rate than did the attendants on the hospital ward. A tentative hypothesis was advanced that his mother and other previous caregivers may not have taken the longer time for feeding Oscar that he required and that they were "misreading" the cues he was exhibiting. Indeed, Oscar may have been reacting to an attempt to hurry through his meal by refusing food and fussing. The mother was instructed to take more time and allow Oscar to pace himself, but without letting his initial refusals terminate the meal. Upon hospital discharge, Oscar was eating all of the food prepared for him regardless of who fed him.

A similar case of food refusal was a 4-year-old child who had been fed liquids via a nasogastric tube for much of his life. When mouth feeding was attempted, the boy resisted by fighting or vomiting. Observation indicated that the boy enjoyed being pushed in a pedal car around the hospital ward. We implemented a reward program by withholding the car until mealtimes, placing him in it, and pushing the car only when food had been swallowed and kept down. A schedule was followed of introducing greater quantities of food ranging in texture initially from melted ice cream and applesauce to ground beef and cheese and eventually to raw carrots. At discharge from the hospital, the boy was generally eating most items in a meal, but was allowed to exercise some acceptable vetoes to certain foods he disliked. These types of cases exemplify reward programs for food refusal.

On the other hand, punishment paradigms are occasionally implemented for infant rumination or regurgitation of food and liquid. This condition is potentially life-threatening. Whereas some successful interventions have relied upon mild electric shock upon rumination (Linscheid & Cunningham, 1977), other practitioners have used contingent squirts of lemon juice or tabasco sauce into the infant's mouth (Becker, Turner, & Sajwaj, 1978). Cases of psychogenic vomiting in older children (vomiting without a physical basis such as chemotherapy or illness) have been similarly treated by electroshock techniques or time-out procedures (Ingersoll & Curry, 1977; Wright & Thalassinos, 1973).

Related to feeding disturbances are acute disruptions of other consummatory responses—namely pill and medication swallowing. A child's refusal to take drugs through the mouth can lead to serious complications. In procedures similar to those used for food refusal, pediatric psychologists have devised reward strategies for shaping, modeling, and reinforcing pill swallowing (Blount, Dahlquist, Baer, & Wuori, 1984; Funk et al., 1984). Although not an acute physical disorder per se, the phenomenon of refusal to consume medicinal drugs is so similar as to warrant inclusion here.

CHRONIC PHYSICAL DISORDERS

Some physical disorders are long-term or lifelong problems that require considerable adjustment for children and their families. These chronic conditions include both diseases and handicaps, such as juvenile diabetes, hemophilia, cancer, heart disease, cystic fibrosis, orthopedic handicaps, and brain damage (see Wright et al., 1979). Medical advancements have extended the lives of many children who previously would have died. The quality of life for many chronically ill children has been improved. With these advances has come an increase in the number of children with chronic disabilities requiring various types of psychological assistance. About 10% of all children in the United States have physical health disorders (Willis, Culbertson, & Mertens, 1984).

Pediatric psychological consultation is often helpful at the point of diagnosis of a chronic condition, during initial medical treatments, at changes in development and treatment, for problems of compliance, and, if applicable, during terminal stages of a fatal illness. Pediatric psychology practitioners will receive referrals for assessment and intervention for a number of chronic physical conditions. As always with a medical disorder, referral to a pediatric text (see chapter 5) or asking questions of the medical staff will be most useful for basic information on the disorder itself. Overviews to psychosocial assessment in chronic disorders are provided by Bronheim and Jacobstein (1984), and Willis et al. (1984).

Among the many aspects of chronic disorders relevant to the psychological practitioner's role, three stand out as particularly important. These are the adjustment of the child and family, the acceptance of the child's peers, and the compliance of the child and family to the medical treatment.

Adjustment

Chronic illness or handicap places special stresses on children and families. These stresses include anxieties over the meaning of a diagnosis, over physical symptoms and medical treatments, over disruption of family life, and about the future (Drotar, Crawford, & Ganofsky, 1984). There has been considerable debate over whether chronically ill children are more maladjusted than physically normal children. Most practitioners' attention and early research studies focused on the problems and poor adjustment of these children. For example, it was suggested that children with cystic fibrosis had more feelings of anxiety, depression, insecurity, and inadequacy. Drotar et al. (1984) summarize the general findings of more recent research with regard to chronic illness:

> (1) the personality and adjustment strengths of chronically ill children outweigh their deficits, (2) for the most part, chronically ill children resemble their physically healthy peers with respect to mental health, (3) chronic illness is best construed as a life stressor which contributes to additional health risk, but is not a primary cause of adjustment problems. (pp. 237-238)

Thus, to return to the cystic fibrosis example, researchers have now concluded that there is no increased emotional disturbance or significant family impairment (e.g., Drotar et al., 1981). Diabetic children similarly are found to be relatively well-adjusted (Sullivan, 1979a, 1979b). Current thinking now suggests that psychological interventions should strive to enhance the coping behavior of chronically ill children and their families rather than just react to maladjustment when it occurs. The newer focus for research and for practitioners' attention is to identify effective coping strategies in chronically ill children and decide how to build on them. Drotar et al. (1984), representing this more current orientation, outlined the role for the pediatric psychologist as helping to enhance the competence of children and families in (a) mastering anxiety associated with physical conditions and its treatment, (b) achieving understanding about the condition and the requisite treatment compliance, (c) integrating the condition into ongoing family life, and (d) adapting to different settings and people (schools, hospitals, peers). This is not to suggest that there are no problems; there are. However, this newer model recasts the situation from a deficit orientation to a competence one.

The practitioner can assist in these enhancement or mental health promotion efforts by being available to children and parents on a continual basis, encouraging active exchanges of information and feelings, involving the family as active participants in treatment, and advocating on behalf of the child and family within a hospital or with another agency. The family is increasingly recognized as a most appropriate context for psychological intervention and preventive work.

As an example of mental health intervention with families, Stabler, Fernald, Johnson, Johnson, and Ryan (1981) developed a supportive program for parents of children with cystic fibrosis. Parent groups were organized to meet in conjunction with regularly scheduled appointments for their children's medical care. Over a period of time, the groups viewed a film on life with the disease and were given information on child development, nutrition, and physical therapy. Presentations of information were made by a pediatrician, genetic counselor, nutritionist, and physical therapist. Group leaders then promoted discussions about the presented material. Through this group process, parents became more knowledgeable about the biomedical issues before being able to turn their attention to psychosocial issues.

Other psychological interventions with the adjustment of chronically ill children have included structured family therapy. Families have also been the focus for psychological intervention with congenital heart disease, juvenile diabetes, neurological disorders, and many others. Adjustment to a chronic condition is a rather amorphous concept and is a continual process with developmental involvement. As illustrated in this section, pediatric psychologists can provide considerable assistance in the enhancement of adjustment.

Acceptance by Peers

If getting sick children and their families to adjust to a chronic physical disorder is a primary task, an immediate secondary one is to get other children to accept ill or handicapped children (Perlman & Routh, 1980; Roberts, Beidleman, & Wurtele, 1981; Roberts, Johnson, & Beidleman, 1984). A number of research reports indicate that children with chronic illness experience problems with peer rejection (see review in Potter & Roberts, 1984). Several factors appear to influence children's perceptions of their chronically ill peers, including observability of the child's disease or handicap, cognitive development of the peers, familiarity or direct experience with another person with the disorder, and the degree to which the nondisordered children have been assisted in acquiring an understanding of the disorders. Some practitioners, for example, suggest that the severity of the symptom and the degree to which an impairment interferes with class activities will influence peer acceptance. Cognitive development plays a role through the sophistication of the children in comprehending and benefiting from experience and information regarding disordered children.

Helping children to understand chronic conditions can have positive impact. First, for the sick child, construction of explanations about disorders at a level appropriate to the patient's cognitive development might improve medical compliance and lessen anxiety. Unfortunately, too many pediatricians still deal primarily with parents and exclude children from understanding and participating in the management of their illness. A second impact would be to influence the nondisordered peers' understanding and, thereby, improve their acceptance of disordered children. Positive peer perception and reactions can have a significant impact on the afflicted child's psychological adjustment and self-acceptance.

A few strategies and guidelines have been proposed by psychologists for explaining illness to children at different ages. Bibace and Walsh (1980), for example, propose the use of broad categories of children's explanations in determining how best to approach the child. In terms of Piagetian notions of cognitive development, preoperational children (generally ages 2 to 7 years) do not abstract well and interpret illness explanation in global, almost magical, terms. Concrete operational children (7 to 11 years) focus on the concrete environment with illness based on contamination—illness is contracted either through contact with the person or object or by doing harmful actions. Whitt, Dykstra, and Taylor (1979) propose the use of metaphorical explanations, especially when dealing with young children. Metaphors relate abstract processes to observable activities with which a child would be familiar. For example, epilepsy is like a telephone wrong number and diabetes is like a malfunctioning car engine (Potter & Roberts, 1984). The psychologist often will be called in to assist in developing appropriate explanations of chronic physical disorders to the afflicted child, to the family, and, often, to peers when starting a transition back to school and normal activities ("mainstreaming").

Compliance

Treatment regimens for chronic illness are often complex, time consuming, and continual, yet are necessary to maintain reasonably good health of the child. Nonadherence with a prescribed regimen is a major concern for all of medicine. Although this noncompliance may seem to be less of a problem for pediatrics because children are supposedly under the control of adults, rates of children's noncompliance with medical regimens are high, ranging up to 82% (Roberts & Wurtele, 1980). The noncompliance may consist of not taking medications, altering diets, or not doing monitoring tests or prescribed exercises. Very simply, noncompliance is the patient's not doing what he or she needs to do in order to maintain a level of health. Because noncompliance is increasingly recognized as a behavioral problem, pediatric psychologists are receiving larger numbers of referrals for it. An extensive literature on the problem is growing even larger. With chronic physical disorders, noncompliance may take on life-threatening implications as in the case of children with cancer — a situation in which 67% of the children in one study stopped taking prescribed medication (Smith, Rosen, Trueworthy, & Lowman, 1979).

Amy (Case 4 in chapter 1) was a 9-year-old child noncompliant with her diabetes treatment regimen. The psychologists had to intervene with written instructions explaining the diabetic regimen of food exchange and diet. Additionally, a point system was devised to reward Amy for following the regimen established by her pediatrician (Lowe & Lutzker, 1979).

Similarly, another pediatric psychologist and pediatrician designed a token reinforcement system for maintenance of special diets for children on a hemodialysis unit (Magrab & Papadopoulou, 1977). After each successful dialysis session, points were awarded depending on measures of acceptable body weight (rather than focusing on eating habits, amounts, or types of food.) The points were recorded and at the end of each week the patients exchanged them for prizes and privileges. The program resulted in reductions in the average weight gain between dialysis sessions and in the degree of weight fluctuation.

In an application with asthmatic children, psychologists taught them how to use bronchodilators in inhalation therapy by training facial posturing, proper eye fixation, and diaphragmatic responses. When these target behaviors were contingently rewarded with tokens redeemable for gifts, the children exhibited the appropriate responses. These behaviors generalized to other situations and were maintained over time (Renne & Creer, 1976). Physically disabled or handicapped children typically have exercise regimes prescribed for rehabilitation.

In an outpatient setting, La Greca and Ottinger (1979) describe a psychological intervention with a young girl's resistance to physical therapy exercises prescribed for muscle stretching associated with cerebral palsy. The exercises were necessary on a daily basis for leg and hip muscles. The psychologists first taught her progressive muscle relaxation to reduce anxiety during the exercises. The girl self-monitored her exercising sessions by recording the time, antecedent activities, reactions during the session, and feelings afterwards. Her parents praised her when she completed a set of exercises, but no additional reinforcement was offered. Compliance with the regimen increased from very few sessions per week to almost daily exercises.

Other pediatric psychologists have successfully trained parents to be physical therapists with their physically handicapped children. Gross, Eudy, and Drabman (1982) trained parents to increase appropriate movement of their children's joints. The children had diagnoses of cerebral palsy, hemiparesis following encephalitis, and quadriparesis subsequent to premature birth complications. Parents were trained through modeling of the physical therapist for prompting and rewarding the children for arm extension (the targeted response). Incorporation of parents in the physical therapy produced significant gains.

There are many such opportunities in which pediatric psychologists can provide consultation and intervention for enhancing compliance with treatments for chronic disorders, as exemplified by these reports with illness and handicaps. Depending on the consultation arrangement, the practitioner can innovate new compliance strategies for particular problems or apply existing conceptualizations.

PSYCHOSOMATIC DISORDERS

Pediatricians and psychologists have long recognized the relationship between physical and psychological factors in children's health. The classification of psychosomatic disorders has been used to describe physical problems caused by emotional disturbance. Wright (1977, 1979b) recommended expanding this category to include physical problems caused by difficulties in learning, development, and personality in addition to the psychological effects resulting from physical illness. This definition greatly expands the rubric of psychosomaticism to well over 100 identified disorders affecting large numbers of children in pediatric settings.

In Wright's model, problems include: (a) physical symptoms produced by psychological problems or stress, such as psychogenic asthma, vomiting, recurrent pain, and ulcerative colitis; (b) physical problems caused or maintained by faulty learning history or developmental anomalies, such as encopresis, enuresis, psychogenic seizures, or tracheotomy addiction; and (c) psychological problems associated with or following medical disorders, such as noncompliance with medical regimens and psychological maladjustment to chronic disease. This expanded model may be overinclusive compared to more traditional interpretations of psychosomatic disorders in that it includes conditions typically categorized under other labels. As many of the disorders noted in the three parts of the model are covered in other places in this book (e.g., encopresis, adjustment to chronic illness), this section will describe pediatric psychology practice as it relates to psychogenic (or psychologically caused) physical disorders of pain and vomiting.

Before turning to these, however, the practitioner should be alerted to one hindrance to practice with these disorders. "Psychosomatic" is often used by physicians, and interpreted by parents, to mean "the problem is all in the head" (Lyman & Roberts, 1984). Similarly, "hypochondriac" may be used to mean psychosomatic. These term usages often impede communication. They may also hinder psychological interventions when the practitioner meets with parents who have been poorly prepared by the pediatrician for consultation with a mental health professional. Parental resistance and denial may frustrate the psychologist. Walker (1979a), for example, reports that some physicians use the acronym CRAP (Chronic Recurrent Abdominal Pain) for pain complaints without apparent physical cause. This demeaning and unreasonable physician attitude probably should be the first target for a diplomatic, but focused, intervention by the pediatric psychologist to help make later patient interventions more productive.

Reinterpretation of symptoms and disorders, without the use of such regressive labels as CRAP or hypochondriasis, into "behavioral habits" or "reactions to stress" often helps. Lyman and Roberts (1984) and Wright (1978a) have outlined steps for a comprehensive assessment of psychosomatic disorders. Wright et al. (1979) described detailed diagnosis and treatment approaches for many specific disorders. In all cases, proper ruling out of physical causes for psychosomatic disorders should be carefully considered by the physician before pediatric psychological intervention.

Psychogenic Pain

Varni, Katz, and Dash (1982) describe four types of pain in children: (a) pain resulting from a disease, (b) pain resulting from injury or trauma, (c) pain resulting from medical or dental procedures, and (d) pain with no associated and defined diseases or injury. Although psychology has something to offer the first three pain categories, it is the fourth that typically is labeled psychogenic pain. The DSM-III category for psychogenic pain disorder is the situation with "a clinical picture in which the predominant feature is the complaint of pain, in the absence of adequate physical findings and in association with evidence of the etiologic role of psychological factors. The disturbance is not due to any other mental disorder" (American Psychiatric Association, 1980, p. 247). Even with this definition indicating there is no physical cause for the pain complaint, we should remember that pain is a very real phenomenon and that in children, as well as adults, psychogenic pain can hurt.

There are several conceptualizations about the meaning of pain and its etiology, each leading to particular types of interventions (Kenny, Bergey, & Young-Hyman, 1983; Lavigne & Burns, 1981; Wright et al., 1979). Additionally, several good conceptualizations exist for assessing pain in children that may lead to a diagnosis of psychogenic pain (e.g., McGrath, Johnson et al., 1985). For example, Green (1983) lists the types of personal, developmental, and family stresses that need to be examined in practitioners' interviews, including separation experiences (e.g., death of relative, divorce), family illness or handicaps (e.g., chronic physical disorders, psychological problems), marital discord, child's difficulty in expression of affect, school problems, sexuality concerns, poor parent–child interactions, and difficulty in peer friendships.

Patrick McGrath and his colleagues have outlined some useful guidelines for psychologists in helping children cope with "chronic benign intractable pain" (McGrath, Dunn-Geier et al., 1985). They use this category for children who have recurrent pains, such as headaches (migraines), limb pain, stomachaches, and chest pains, that are benign or without an apparent underlying physical disorder. Estimates of prevalence of pain complaints indicate fairly high numbers of children exhibit this type of pain. Most of the children with chronic pain are able to cope fairly well. However, a number of children have difficulties with school attendance and maintaining social activities and become too attentive to their pain. They may overly involve their families, seek unnecessary medical treatments, and seek out a multitude of physicians. The guidelines that these practitioners outline can be used with those children exhibiting a variety of pain complaints who are coping poorly with the pain and also with the families' coping problems.

First, they recommend that the psychologist conduct a psychosocial assessment shortly after the patient presents with pain complaints, rather than have the psychologist's involvement come after other diagnostic procedures have failed to find physical causes. Psychosocial assessment is especially necessary when the child (or family) is not coping well. Assessment should include interviewing, home recordkeeping, and behavioral observations. They note that psychological tests have not been widely used in this area. McGrath et al. suggest that early assessment has the advantages of not allowing problems to become too firmly entrenched and of keeping the psychologist's procedures intertwined concurrently with the physician's diagnostic workup. Close liaison is particularly important in this disorder.

The second guideline states that all parties should avoid making a dichotomy between organic causes and psychogenic causes of pain. They note that when emphasis is given to the psychogenic nature of pain, it may be out of the frustration of the medical practitioner for failing to find a physical cause. This, however, does not automatically "rule in" psychological causation. Similarly, guideline 8 suggests that professionals avoid blaming the patient or the family for the pain.

Such blaming may arise from professional frustrations with intractable patients, but does not lead to successful remediation of the problem. Additionally, making an uncoordinated psychological referral and ascribing psychogenic labels to the pain might alienate the patient and family.

Guideline 3 holds that the psychologist should establish the "context and meaning of the pain," that is, the psychologist should determine the relationship between life events and pain complaints. They recommend that observation of pain episodes and having the parents or child keep incident records or diaries can help establish any relationships. As noted earlier in this chapter, examining the Antecedents-Behavior-Consequences relationship may lead to a better understanding of the dynamics of a situation. The practitioner can interview the child and parents to find out what they think about the pain and its causes. The authors have found in their practice that it is rarely helpful to doubt the validity of a pain complaint. Downplaying the concerns actually might lead to an increase in complaints as the patient tries to prove the "realness" of it. Necessary trust and rapport between patient and practitioner might be jeopardized.

The fourth guideline of McGrath et al. emphasizes the coping with, not the curing of, the pain as an ultimate goal. The psychologist can help these families best by focusing on the ways in which the child might deal appropriately with the pain when it occurs and how the child can maintain regular activities around it. Similarly, guideline 5 suggests focusing on the family's strengths rather than on the pathological aspects of the family or the pain complaint.

As the child spends a great deal of time in school, the next guideline (6) urges that the school situation be carefully investigated. School-related stresses, such as bullies, peer rejection, fear of failure, among others, may be contributing to the pain complaints. McGrath et al., in their guideline 7, further suggest that the practitioner teach coping skills so that the child and family will achieve a sense of control over the problem in addition to an actual reduction in pain. They cite various modalities for teaching coping skills, including cognitive restructuring, hypnosis, and relaxation training.

Finally, in guideline 9, they recommend that health professionals try to understand without pitying the noncoping child. They suggest that the practitioner model firm and realistic expectations while providing short-term goals through shaping of more appropriate behavior when necessary. These authors have found that interdisciplinary efforts are essential for helping families of children with chronic benign intractable pain. Mental health and medical practitioners must often shift roles and work closely in these situations.

The behavioral approach to psychogenic pain generally meets the orientation of pediatric psychology toward efficacy, brevity, and, therefore, pragmatism. Fordyce (1976) presents the operant view that some pains are environmentally influenced by reinforcement such as getting out of school or parental attention. In the case of Karen, noted in chapter 1 (Case 2), no organic cause could be determined for her persistent and severe stomach pains. Karen's pain complaints were viewed as being reinforced by missing school, increased attention by the mother, and access to television and toys. The behavioral intervention consisted of time-out procedures contingent upon Karen's report of pain (e.g., rest in bed, no television or toys, and minimal parent interaction). This was sequentially implemented at home and then at school. Karen gradually reduced her pain reports (Miller & Kratochwill, 1979). A similar conceptualization was advanced for another recurrent abdominal pain case reported by Sank and Biglan (1974), with points (later changed for money) awarded for periods of time without complaints and time-out for pain reports.

As noted in chapter 2, the cases of pain reports by Karen (Miller & Kratochwill, 1979) and Stephen (Stabler, 1979) are superficially similar in that both patients complained of stomach pain for which no physical cause could be found. Indeed, both cases rightfully deserve the diagnosis of psychogenic pain disorder. Karen's complaints appeared to be reinforced. In contrast to Karen, though, Stephen's pain was conceptualized as stress resulting through a different etiology. Stephen was viewed as having difficulty expressing affect, especially in relation to the death of his father from stomach cancer, and he coped by defense mechanisms of repression and denial. Supportive counseling led to symptom abatement. Therefore, a strict behavioral orientation for psychogenic pain is not reflected in pediatric psychology.

Psychogenic Vomiting

As noted in the section on acute physical disorders, there are feeding disturbances in which an infant may ruminate or spit up the entire contents of the stomach or an older child may vomit ("emesis" in medical jargon) without any medical reason such as food poisoning or influenza. Sibinga (1983) notes that such episodes have been termed cyclic, episodic, hysterical, and habitual vomiting, in addition to psychogenic vomiting.

Davis and Cuvo (1980) conceptualized these disorders under an operant behavioral rubric, that is, infant rumination and child vomiting often result in reinforcement of the child through adult attention and avoidance of disliked activities. Following this orientation, behavioral approaches for rumination have included lemon juice or tabasco sauce in the mouth (e.g., Becker et al., 1978), although success is not always reported (see Lavigne & Burns, 1981). Positive reinforcement strategies have been employed to increase nonvomiting behaviors, with extinction or punishment for vomiting episodes. Munford and Pally (1979) shifted environment reinforcement from the vomiting acts to more positive behaviors in order to eliminate vomiting in an 11-year-old child.

In general, psychogenic vomiting may be distinguished from the "purging" or self-induced vomiting associated with bulimia and anorexia nervosa, although some resemblances are notable. Due to the complexity of these related disorders, the practitioner may want to refer to another book in this series (Weiss, Katzman, & Wolchik, 1985).

Other Psychogenic Disorders

There are many other pediatric problems categorized as psychosomatic. These include disorders whose physical symptoms are either exacerbated by stress or totally caused by stress.

Asthma

Intractable asthma is one problem in which there is a basic physiological factor, such as infection, allergies, or immunological and endocrine factors, causing difficulty in breathing (Hirsch & Russo, 1983). Stress resulting from different sources generally is thought to influence asthmatic attacks. In fact, there are some cases where emotional factors appear to be the primary cause. Some physicians often speculate about psychogenic factors due to their own difficulties in treating asthma with medical approaches. (See reviews in Falliers, 1983, and Wright et al., 1979, about such psychosocial factors as maternal overprotection, maternal rejection, and family conflicts.)

The pediatric psychologist may implement a variety of treatment modalities in conjunction with ongoing medical treatment, such as reinforcement for proper use of bronchodilator medication inhaled through nebulizers. Some practitioners have combined biofeedback and relaxation in a systematic desensitization program to decrease the anxiety associated with asthma attacks (Feldman, 1976). Other psychological practitioners have worked on increasing compliance with the medical regimen and on decreasing hospitalization (Creer, Renne, & Christian, 1976; Renne & Creer, 1976). Family therapy is sometimes required for cases of unresolved conflicts (Liebman, Minuchin, & Baker, 1974). "Parentectomy" is an unfortunate term used by some professionals for separating asthmatic children and their families over a long term. This separation through long-term hospitalization, residential, or foster-care placement is claimed to be successful in alleviating asthma symptoms for severe cases (Liebman et al., 1974; Prugh, 1983). Asthma is clearly a psychosomatic disorder with a multitude of possible roles for the practitioner. The pediatric psychologist may find the pediatrician all too willing to refer his or her more frustrating asthma cases.

Ulcerative Colitis

Ulcerative colitis is a classic instance of a psychosomatic disorder (see review by Lavigne & Burns, 1981) in which the colon becomes inflamed with concomitant diarrhea containing blood and mucus. This and related conditions (inflammatory bowel disease, mucous colitis, spastic colon) often appear in school-age children and seem related to emotional conflict.

Similarly, ulcers, some skin disorders such as eczema, some types of headaches, and some seizure disorders have psychophysiological bases (Prugh, 1983; Wright et al., 1979). Because of the interaction of physical *and* psychological factors, when called in to consult on such cases, the practitioner is well-advised to gain an understanding of the physical aspects of the problem by checking a pediatric textbook (see chapter 5) before attempting assessment and intervention with psychosomatic disorders (Lyman & Roberts, 1984).

DEVELOPMENTAL DISORDERS

A large segment of pediatric psychology practice deals with developmental disorders or disabilities, the category of problems in which the normal processes of physical, emotional, and intellectual growth are delayed. Typically, cases are first seen as evaluation referrals because a parent or pediatrician suspects the child is not developing normally. A few cases may turn out to be situations where the parent has unreal expectations for the child's development. Educative interventions about normal development and children's behavior often help realign parental expectations for healthy development. Often, however, suspicions of delayed development are borne out by the evaluation using tests such as the Bayley Scales of Infant Development. In these cases, the pediatric psychologist not only must assess the current status, but must also inform the parents of the diagnosis/prognosis and develop plans for stimulation and intervention.

The more frequent developmental disorders are failure to thrive, autism, and mental retardation. Some psychologists would put hyperactivity problems in this category as well. Excellent chapters in the *Encyclopedia of Pediatric Psychology* on developmental assessment and developmental intervention provide general coverage of these areas (Wright et al., 1979).

Failure to Thrive

Failure to thrive is the lack of growth in an infant without evidence of physical cause (Roberts & Maddux, 1982). An infant is commonly considered to exhibit failure to thrive if he or she falls below the 3rd percentile in weight (and sometimes considerations of height and head circumference are included). These factors are typically measured on pediatric growth charts (Wright, 1978a). Other characteristics include weight loss or poor weight gain, feeding difficulties or food refusal, spitting up, vomiting, diarrhea, delayed developmental milestones, and withdrawal or lethargy. However, these are not always present. Among the medical etiologies commonly ruled out in the diagnostic process are malabsorption, endocrine disorders, allergies, worms, renal disorders, chronic infections, and diabetes. Tertiary care settings (e.g., referrals at children's hospitals) have been the traditional resource for failure-to-thrive infants, although they do appear in emergency rooms of general hospitals and in public health clinics.

Several conceptualizations regarding the psychosocial etiology of failure to thrive have been proposed. These have historically been subsumed under the labels of social, environmental, or maternal deprivation. However, this conceptualization has been criticized for being inadequate (Rutter, 1979). Criticism notwithstanding, it is common to find in a hospitalized infant's medical chart the diagnosis "failure to thrive secondary to maternal deprivation syndrome." A more recent psychosocial conceptualization describes nonorganic failure to thrive and its concomitants as a complex problem requiring comprehensive therapeutic intervention involving pediatric psychologists, pediatricians, and other health-care professionals (Roberts & Horner, 1979; Roberts & Maddux, 1982). The many causative factors involved in failure to thrive can be classified into three major categories: (a) psychological/emotional factors, (b) educational factors, and (c) environmental factors.

Within the category of psychological/emotional factors are such characteristics as the care-giver's (most often the mother) psychological functioning, including long-standing behavior patterns, attitudes, personality, and interaction styles. Mothers of failure-to-thrive infants often exhibit psychological problems, including passivity, depression, anger, anxiety, and helplessness. These and other problems heighten the probability of difficulties in coping successfully with the normal problems of child care. The parent may have difficulty in recognizing the infant's physical and psychological needs or may not develop the emotional attachment to the child that is important for heathy development. The care-giver may be experiencing situation-specific stress reactions to poor marital relationships and financial difficulties. The lack of family stability impedes the care and stimulation of the child. Also of concern are attitudes and behavior of the care-giver concerning the child. For example, the mother may mistakenly attribute intentionality to the infant's behavior such as spitting up or may misinterpret crying. The mother may expect the child to think like an adult and to understand the mother and respond to her as another adult would.

A second major category in failure to thrive is educational factors. Parents of these infants are often ignorant of the proper methods and skills of child care. They lack information about child behavior that would facilitate the development of a healthy relationship between care-giver and child. Some care-givers employ inappropriate feeding procedures, such as spoon feeding before the child is developmentally ready, force feeding, giving the wrong types of food, or giving improper amounts of food. A care-giver may also be thwarted by environmental factors that are beyond immediate control, such as financial problems, housing, and medical care.

This conceptualization of failure to thrive calls attention to the complex developmental factors comprising the syndrome. This formulation by Roberts and Maddux (1982) emphasizes that interventions must be made on all factors rather than restricting the focus to the mother. Professionals need to treat more than just one problem because, if ignored, the overwhelming influence of the other factors will not subside, and the problems will continue. A major role can be played by pediatric psychology in the treatment interventions.

The case of Oscar, a 5-month-old infant (Case 1, chapter 1), illustrates the application of this conceptualization and the necessity of comprehensive treatment for failure to thrive (Roberts & Horner, 1979). He was below the 3rd percentile on the growth charts. After all diagnostic tests were completed to rule out other disorders and confirm the failure-to-thrive diagnosis, various hospital units became involved in Oscar's treatment. The occupational therapy department conducted several assessments of Oscar's progress using the DDST and identified problems in the area of gross motor ability. Daily therapeutic sessions with Oscar were made while he was an inpatient, followed by twice weekly therapies as an outpatient. His mother attended most of the sessions for instruction in how to stimulate him. A pediatric nurse practitioner (PNP) maintained contact with the mother and child in an outpatient clinic for medical follow-up. The PNP educated the mother in childrearing and health practices and visited the home to enhance compliance and family acceptance and to provide supportive counseling for problems in the parents' lives as needed. The psychology division provided individual psychotherapy for his mother's depression using a cognitive–behavioral treatment approach. Additionally, while Oscar was still hospitalized, the pediatric psychology division completed a behavioral assessment and intervention program for his feeding problems (this was detailed in the previous section on acute physical disorders). Pediatric psychology also made baseline and follow-up evaluations of Oscar's mental and motor development using the Bayley Scales of Infant Development. The initial assessment revealed that Oscar was functioning generally 3 months below his age level and was developmentally delayed in several areas. Over time, and with the intensive interventions, Oscar's scores on the Bayley indices increased until he was functioning at his age level (Roberts & Horner, 1979).

Autism and Mental Retardation

These two disorders are particularly complex to diagnose and treat. In particular, the two disorders need to be differentially diagnosed relative to each other, to developmental language disability, and to childhood schizophrenia. Dawson and Mesibov (1983) discuss the research and clinical base for this differentiation. The DSM-III outlines the characteristics of autism, including six criteria: (a) onset of condition before age 30 months, (b) pervasive lack of responsiveness to others, (c) major deficits in language abilities, (d) peculiar speech patterns when language is present, (e) bizarre responses to environment, and (f) no delusions, hallucinations, or other loose associations (American Psychiatric Association, 1980). Mental retardation generally involves subaverage intellectual functioning and deficits in adaptive behavior (Cleland, 1983).

Once a definitive diagnosis of autism is made, the communication of the diagnosis and its meaning becomes critical. When a child is diagnosed with a developmental disorder such as autism, the manner in which the parents are counseled has ramifications for their understanding of the problem, acceptance of the child, adjustment to the diagnosis, and eventual participation in treatment. Pediatric psychologists can assist in helping parents and families during the diagnostic evaluation period and in the feedback about what was learned in the assessment.

Sam Morgan (1984) has prepared a useful set of guidelines for helping people understand the diagnosis of autism. First, the professionals, including the pediatric psychologist, should become knowledgeable about recent findings in autism, such as the new emphasis on cognitive impairment rather than abnormal affective development. Second, the counselor should avoid jargon and labels and especially avoid "casting blame" on the parents for the disorder either directly or by implication, such as recommending parental psychotherapy. (There is currently no evidence that parents cause autism). Third, the counselor should realistically inform the parents about the disorder, providing practical advice and supportive counseling for the future care of the child. Fourth, the counselor can solicit the parents' estimate of their child's functioning (e.g., social, cognitive, motor, self-help, and intellectual functioning). These can be incorporated into discussions of the adaptive abilities that may have been observed during the assessment because impairments usually have been observed by the parents; the test data can confirm these. Fifth, Morgan recommends that the impairments be communicated through interpretable approximations and ranges, for example, "the child functions in some ways at the 4-year level." The relative strengths and weaknesses for the child should be stressed because autistic children show variability in areas of impaired functioning.

Finally, the counselor should provide information on the future of the child. This must be tentative because prognosis is not clear-cut. Autism is a severe and chronic disorder, and independent functioning as an adult is rare. However, these factors should be tempered by statements that enrollment in a systematic educational and behavioral program will improve chances of better adjustment. Morgan (1984) further suggests that parents be allowed a chance to ventilate their feelings, often of anger, frustration, and depression.

The pediatric psychologist whose practice might involve diagnosis of developmental disorders will find Morgan's guidelines quite useful. I have also found Harriet Rheingold's (1945) classic paper to be most helpful in interpreting mental retardation to parents. If the informing and counseling stage is handled adroitly for developmental disorders, later pediatric, educational, and behavioral interventions will be facilitated.

PSYCHOLOGICAL-BEHAVIORAL PROBLEMS

A large proportion of the cases seen in pediatric psychology services, as depicted in Table 2.1 of chapter 2, involve negative behavior, school, and personality problems. These types of problems are also frequently seen in traditional clinical child psychology practices, and thus, are not unique to pediatric psychology. However, because they comprise large numbers of cases seen through pediatric referrals, such behavioral problems are important. If one wanted to handle these patients, a practice could be devoted almost exclusively to them without reference to other aspects of pediatric psychology. In that situation, the practice is probably less pediatric psychology than it is clinical child psychology.

Noncompliance

Behavioral problems of noncompliance are covered by a vast and growing literature that is readily adaptable by the pediatric psychologist (Forehand & McMahon, 1981; Patterson, 1982). Because of this availability, I will not describe these behavioral approaches, but will discuss how the interventions can be implemented in pediatric settings.

As noted in chapter 3, a consultative role can be taken by the pediatric psychologist through independent functions and indirect consultation. Within the independent functions model, for example, the noncompliance problems may be targeted through parent-training groups conducted by the psychologist. These groups provide the vehicle for giving information on child management techniques through discussions by parents about their attempts to use them (Forgatch & Toobert, 1979). The groups can be held in the pediatrician's practice, in a psychological clinic, or in public facilities. Topics can include the use of time-out and ignoring for misbehavior and noncompliance and rewards and attention for positive behaviors. Parent-training groups are also useful for specialized behavioral management of children with medical disorders such as asthma, leukemia, diabetes, and hyperactivity. Of course, parent education also can take place in individual treatment outside the medical setting (Eyberg & Matarazzo, 1980).

Carolyn Schroeder's pediatric psychology practice within a multispecialty clinic illustrates the frequent behavioral interventions for noncompliance problems (Schroeder, 1979). Table 2.1 in chapter 2 depicts the high percentage of referrals for negative behaviors in pediatric psychology practices, especially in Schroeder's setting (Kanoy & Schroeder, 1985). Schroeder and her colleagues provide parent consultation through the call in/come in service, with individual appointments available for major problems. This service uses environmental changes, such as punishing and ignoring negative behaviors while rewarding and encouraging positive behaviors. This independent functions consultation appears to be a highly effective, economical approach to handling referrals via pediatric offices.

Behavioral noncompliance has also been treated through the indirect psychological consultation model. As noted in chapter 3, pediatricians and their staffs can be trained to provide basic parent education for managing children (Harper, 1975). This can be accomplished through discussion and written handouts or protocols (see Table 3.1 in chapter 3). For example, Drabman and Rosenbaum (1980) describe for pediatricians how to counsel parents on the child behavior problems of early morning dawdling and misbehavior away from home (Drabman & Jarvie, 1977). With a psychologist's assistance, the pediatrician can counsel the parents about the use of time-out and response–cost procedures (removal of a desired activity). The pediatrician and clinic staff also can provide psychologist-developed protocols for bedtime problems and temper tantrums (Rainey & Christophersen, 1976), for example, to parents who report this type of noncompliance. These child-management interventions easily can be made during well-child visits when many nonmedical problems are reported by parents. Pediatric nurse practitioners, in particular, can be trained to provide management counseling, such as for bedtime problems (Rapoff, Christophersen, & Rapoff, 1982). Because behavioral noncompliance problems are such a high-frequency presenting problem in pediatric psychology, the practitioner needs to have ready pragmatic procedures for handling them or for referral to other mental health professionals.

Adjustment to Divorce

Because a pediatrician is often seen as almost a member of the family, he or she is often consulted when family disruption occurs. This may come through direct request by a parent for advice or in the course of a pediatric visit. Frequently, marital distress and divorces occur in relation to terminal illness in the family, so the alert physician is well placed to render assistance. The pediatric psychologist can provide assistance to the pediatrician and staff on how to respond to parents (indirect consultation), as well as when to refer cases of possible extreme family maladjustment (independent functions consultation).

The psychologist can provide background information about the effects of divorce on children and information on custodial arrangements, in addition to counseling parents and children. Much research indicates that there are emotional, behavioral, and cognitive effects on children because of separation and divorce. A number of studies have found that children from divorced families exhibit behavior problems such as aggressiveness, noncompliance, and distractability, particularly in the first year after the divorce (Hetherington, Cox, & Cox, 1979). Children of divorce show emotional reactions ranging from toilet training problems and sleep disturbance to anxiety, depression, and aggression, often over a year after parents' separation (Wallerstein, 1983; Wyman, Cowen, Hightower, & Pedro-Carroll, 1985). Although the psychological effects of divorce are complex and not universal, the divorce situation places the child at risk for psychological problems (Lyman & Roberts, 1985).

Custody and visitation arrangements play an important part in a child's adjustment. Many expert opinions have been ventured on this topic, but very little research has studied it. However, some research is building to support joint custody as a more positive arrangement, where both parents share the responsibility for decision making about the child's situation (Wallerstein, 1983; Wolchik, Braver, & Sandler, 1985). Professional caution is needed to insure that such an arrangement is truly optimal for the child. Greater frequency and duration of visitation with a noncustodial parent have been associated with less stress and greater self-esteem (Wallerstein, 1983).

The psychologist can also provide written material, such as Lee Salk's *What Every Child Would Like His Parents to Know About Divorce* (1978), for parents via the pediatrician. Counseling for the parents can be offered as mediation prior to any decisions and during negotiations on custody. Psychological help for the child can be provided to aid in adjustment. Children's stress reactions may be manifested as physical symptoms requiring conjoint medical and psychological interventions.

PREVENTION

Pediatric psychology has, throughout its development, manifested an orientation to prevention (Roberts, 1986b, 1986c). Such an orientation attempts to take action to avoid development of a problem or disorder and to identify problems early enough to minimize their potential negative outcomes (Peterson & Roberts, in press; Roberts & Peterson, 1984b). However, at times prevention has been minimized in practice in lieu of treatment-oriented activities for already existing problems. Prevention activities in pediatric psychology include applying psychology to the prevention of mental health problems or psychiatric disorders and to the prevention of physical problems such as injuries and illness in childhood. Thus, pediatric psychologists often may become involved in preventing physical and sexual abuse or precluding its reoccurrence (Saslawsky & Wurtele, 1986; Walker, Bonner, & Kaufman, in press).

Working through the pediatrician's initial contacts with a family, the psychologist may provide interventions to prevent emotional and behavioral problems for children whose parents are divorcing. Within hospitals, psychologists have designed programs to prepare children for hospitalization and surgery in order to prevent negative consequences from the medical experience (Elkins & Roberts, 1983). Other interventions use a psychology base to change lifestyles and promote healthy development through nutrition, exercise, and dental care. Childhood is a most appropriate time for prevention—before any onset of problems (Peterson & Roberts, in press; Roberts & Peterson, 1984a).

Medicine, more so than psychology, has adopted a preventive approach intertwined with therapeutic activities. Immunizations for preventing illnesses have contributed greatly to the decline in morbidity and mortality. Consequently, pediatricians are predisposed to thinking preventively. The psychologist can tap this predisposition in implementing prevention programs.

Anticipatory Guidance

Pediatricians use the term "anticipatory guidance" to describe the professional's anticipating common problems and providing counseling and education in advance of any difficulties (Brazelton, 1975; Christophersen & Barnard, 1978; Nelson et al., 1975; Roberts & Wright, 1982). Anticipatory guidance bases counseling on the fact that different-age children have developing abilities and behaviors that require different actions and precautions. Issues of concern range from feeding and nutrition to sibling rivalry and from safe, stimulating toys to behavioral discipline. For example, changes in motoric abilities follow maturational patterns, with predictable changes in increased mobility, thereby increasing the child's risks for injury and disease (Roberts, Maddux, & Wright, 1984).

During well-child visits, the pediatrician describes common hazards associated with each developmental stage. For example, the young infant about to learn to roll over requires supervision when at unsecured heights (e.g., beds or changing tables without railings); the crawling child needs to have the house "poison-proofed," all electrical outlets covered, stairways blocked, cupboards secured, and small objects removed from reach; the walking child requires the care-giver's attention to the higher reaching ability around stoves and cabinets (Dershewitz & Christophersen, 1984). Other anticipatory guidance includes preparatory information on potential changes in sleeping, eating, teething, and reactions to immunizations. Common behavioral problems and changes in psychological abilities also are described before they occur, and the pediatrician offers advice on how to handle them successfully.

When assessing the need for anticipatory guidance, the physician often asks the parent or child to describe a typical day, while being alert to behavioral patterns possibly indicative of more serious problems (Christophersen & Barnard, 1978; Rainey & Christophersen, 1976). This approach will be more productive than just asking if the child is exhibiting any behavioral problems.

The pediatrician or pediatric nurse may also provide information on coping with developmental transitions such as preparing a child for a new sibling, getting ready to start school, or the death of a grandparent. The widely used and recently revised *Dr. Spock's Baby and Child Care* book is a bibliographic source of anticipatory guidance to handle the vast array of medical and psychological concerns in parenting (Spock & Rothenberg, 1985).

Anticipatory guidance relies on the developmental perspective noted in chapter 2, with a particular emphasis on when preventive interventions are most needed (Roberts, Elkins, & Royal, 1984). The pediatric psychologist can provide considerable input to anticipatory guidance in general pediatric practice (Cameron & Rice, 1986).

In hospital settings, anticipatory guidance includes preparing for changes in disease-related effects and enhancing coping to master them (Drotar et al., 1984). For example, physical limitations on activities of the child with cystic fibrosis may

require teaching the patient how to respond to peer questions or teasing. By anticipating changes in social, emotional, and physical needs during adolescence, the
diabetic preadolescent can be given instructions on how to take greater responsibility for diabetic treatment. The side effects of steroids (e.g., puffy faces) given to
enhance organ acceptance in children who have had kidney transplants are upset-
ting to the children and often require preparatory work.

In outpatient practice, the pediatric psychologist can provide child management
information (as in the previously described Carolyn Schroeder call in/come in
service), by protocols (as described in chapter 2), or through bibliographic
resources (described in chapter 5). Additionally, the pediatric psychologist can
conduct programming for preventing psychological disorders and for enhancing
health and safety through psychological applications. Despite the appeal of anticipatory guidance for pediatric practices, my experience indicates that less of it is
done than should be.

Psychological Disorders

Psychological efforts have been made to prevent psychopathology and behavioral problems, including academic difficulties, social skills deficits, hyperactivity,
aggressiveness, and so on (Roberts & Peterson, 1984b). Of additional concern is
the identification of children who are at risk for the development of later problems.
Early identification of these children can be conducted ideally in pediatric
settings.

Hospitalization is one particular life event placing children at risk for emotional
maladjustment (Elkins & Roberts, 1983; Peterson & Brownlee-Duffeck, 1984).
Because this event takes place in medical settings, the involvement of pediatric
psychologists in prevention programming is facilitated. In alliance with nurses
and child-life specialists, psychologists have designed and implemented a number
of different types of programs. Elkins and Roberts (1983) reviewed psychological
preparation programs for pediatric hospitalization. Such programs range from
providing information to encouraging emotional expression, from establishing
relationships of trust and confidence, to providing coping strategies. These efforts
have been communicated through a variety of media, including verbal communication, play therapy, hospital tours, printed materials, and audiovisual materials.
Many children's hospitals provide routine preparation programs for children
scheduled for admission, although some programs are in danger of folding due to
financial cutbacks (Roberts, 1986a).

Ethan Has An Operation is one commercially available film that has received
research validation (Elkins & Roberts, 1985; Melamed & Siegel, 1975). This film
features a boy who is admitted to a hospital for hernia surgery. Specific information about medical procedures is related by hospital staff, and the patient narrates
his own feelings during the film. He expresses some fears, but is portrayed as
successfully coping with the hospital experience. This film has been used by sev-

eral hospitals and is available from the Health Sciences Communication Center (Case Western Reserve University, Cleveland, OH 44106).

A commercially distributed videotape, *Let's Talk About Having An Operation,* features Mr. Rogers, the popular children's television personality (available from Family Communications, 4802 Fifth Avenue, Pittsburgh, PA 15213). Mr. Rogers narrates the tape about a girl who is admitted to the hospital for surgery. He provides information about what children should expect while in the hospital and encourages them to express their feelings in words and play. This videotape has received some research evaluation (Elkins & Roberts, 1985; Klinzing & Klinzing, 1977). These programs are generally conducted with children who are about to be or who are already admitted to the hospital.

We need to be especially careful about how we talk with children when attempting to prepare them for medical events. Even the approach of using metaphors, articulated by Whitt et al. (1979), can be a problem. I observed a child who had been prepared using dolls and puppets for a cardiac catheterization. The patient calmly sat through the explanation of the procedures, which the social worker demonstrated on a doll. In this process, she said that a small tube or hose would be inserted in an artery and put into the heart. The next morning when the aides came to take the boy to surgery, he was found clinging to the underside of the bed, crying, and saying he did not want a garden hose put into his heart.

Another prevention approach has been to prepare children even before they are scheduled for hospitalization admission in a "population-wide" prevention strategy, that is, with children who are well. In my own work, we have developed a slide and audiotape program, *Paul and Dot Have a Hospital Experience,* for reducing medical fears and increasing medical knowledge in nonpatient children (Elkins & Roberts, 1985; Roberts, Wurtele, Boone, Ginther, & Elkins, 1981). This package depicts two children entering a hospital and describes various medical procedures, equipment, and personnel. The children acknowledge anxiety, but are able to overcome it through specific coping strategies such as self-talk and cognitive restructuring. This program was shown to nonpatient children in their school classrooms.

In another preventive program, we assisted in developing an experiential and information project entitled *Let's Pretend Hospital.* This program targeted nonpatient children in a milestone format (i.e., targeting all children at a particular age or developmental stage). The program exposed first-grade children to medical/ hospital events, personnel, and equipment set up in a national guard armory. This mock hospital contains several different units (e.g., admissions, patient's room, surgery) in which the children have "hands-on" experiences with medical apparatus and in which personnel provide information to the children. This pretend hospital for well children was found to reduce medical fears and increase medical knowledge (Elkins & Roberts, 1984).

As illustrated by these programs, prevention approaches can be implemented in hospitals and external settings. The Association for the Care of Children's Health

(ACCH) maintains an excellent compilation of media and resources available for a variety of efforts to alleviate fear and anxiety associated with medical events, settings, and staff (ACCH, 1985). These include special topics of heart catheterization, pediatric intensive care, emergency admissions, chronic illness, and terminal illness, in addition to general hospitalization issues. (This bibliography and other materials on health care for children and families are available from ACCH, 3615 Wisconsin Avenue NW, Washington, DC 20016).

Physical Problems

Pediatric psychologists, due in part to the emphasis in medicine on prevention of disease and injury in childhood, have maintained a number of activities aimed at the prevention of physical problems. A greater impetus comes from the recognition of the importance of improving children's health and safety, and psychology has much to offer this prevention field (Roberts, 1986c; Roberts, Elkins, & Royal, 1984). Professionals increasingly realize that further significant improvement in the quality of human life (physical status, longevity) will not be made by technological advancements, but through individual actions related to behavior and lifestyles. Hence, psychologists are increasingly turning their attention to research and applications for the prevention of injuries and illness.

Psychological principles and techniques find ready application to this problem area. For example, systematic programs have been designed to teach children self-protective behaviors for preventing abduction and molestation (Poche, Brouwer, & Swearingen, 1981), taking emergency actions in home fires and identifying emergency situations (Hillman, Jones, & Farmer, 1986; Jones, Kazdin, & Haney, 1981a, 1981b), crossing streets properly (Yeaton & Bailey, 1978), and brushing teeth (Levy, Lodish, & Pawlack-Floyd, 1982; Murray & Epstein, 1981). Two programs will be detailed here to illustrate preventive actions the pediatric psychologist can make.

Lizette Peterson (1984b, 1984c) developed a *Safe At Home* program to train children who are at home without direct adult supervision — the so-called "latch key" children. These children are at risk for injuries and stress. Peterson's program utilizes behavioral techniques and intensive training on how to: (a) react to such emergencies as a fire, cut hand, or tornado alert; (b) respond to strangers at the door or on the telephone; (c) select nutritious snacks; and (d) select optimal after-school activities. This prevention program demonstrates clear-cut gains in the children's safety behavior (Peterson, Mori, & Scissors, 1986). It is particularly adaptable to implementation in a number of settings.

In another safety-oriented application, my colleagues and I designed and implemented reward-based programs to motivate children's use of car safety systems such as seat belts and safety seats. Virtually all children are at risk for death and injury as passengers in motor vehicles. Between 70–90% of this could be reduced or prevented if children were restrained. Yet, only a minority of children are properly buckled up (Roberts & Turner, 1984). Our safety programs have targeted young children arriving at day-care centers and older children arriving at elementary schools. In one program, tokens for a lottery were given to parents when their children were properly restrained in the car upon arrival at preschools. The winning tokens were redeemable for pizzas, movie passes, chicken dinners, and so forth. Safety seat usage increased significantly (Roberts & Turner, 1986). In two additional projects, it was determined that giving stickers as rewards directly to the preschool children increased their riding safely (Roberts & Layfield, in press) and that having day-care teachers provide the rewards inside the school also was successful (Roberts & Broadbent, 1986).

In a developmental extension, we implemented community-wide interventions (*Buckle Up Bama's Future*) to reward school children for buckling up enroute to their schools (Roberts & Fanurik, 1986; Roberts, Fanurik, & Wilson, 1986). Rewards consisting of stickers, coloring books, bumper stickers, and pizza dinners were provided children who were buckled into safety belts and whose fellow passengers were safely secured. The program evaluation indicated significant increases in the safety behavior.

Another pediatric psychologist, Edward Christophersen, developed a written protocol to provide to parents in order to increase their use of child safety-seats. This protocol emphasizes that safety-seat use increases the child's appropriate behavior, without describing any of the negative consequences of a child riding unsecured in a collision. Some research evaluation has demonstrated that use of this protocol with pediatrician counseling increases safety seat usage (Christophersen & Gyulay, 1981). This program also has been implemented through outpatient pediatric practices (Treiber, 1986). Hospitals can enhance safety seat usage through programs to provide loaned seats to parents and through hospital policies to discharge newborns only into the seats (Christophersen, Sosland-Edelman, & LeClaire, 1985; Roberts & Turner, 1984).

These types of physical health programs move pediatric psychology into the realm of behavioral health—the promotion of health and the prevention of illness and injury (Matarazzo, 1984). Increasing car passenger safety and enhancing children's home safety behavior are just two examples of pediatric psychology practice to protect the health of children. The psychologist's ability to recognize the needs and to innovate in order to meet these needs is the only limitation on successful practice in this area.

Constantly being alert to prevention needs in pediatric psychology will turn up a multitude of opportunities. For example, I attended one medical rounds for a large pediatric ward where there was great concern by the pediatric resident, medical students, and attending physicians over the electrolyte balance and the medical status before discharge of a child who had unintentionally ingested poisons. However, until the psychologists in attendance called it to the group's attention, there was no discussion over how to help the parents change the child's environment to prevent a poisoning reoccurrence. Similar preventive interventions can be made for a variety of hazardous situations such as bathtub drownings, injury while sleeping, and potential lead poisoning, among others.

The American Academy of Pediatrics (AAP) instituted a project in this area called *The Injury Prevention Program* (TIPP), which involves physician-administered safety surveys, pediatric counseling, and one-page handouts in developmental sequences on topics of car injuries, falls, burns, choking, drowning, and poisoning. The AAP also sponsors a *The First Ride . . . A Safe Ride* program with numerous materials on child passenger safety. (Information on these programs can be obtained from AAP, P.O. Box 1034, Evanston, IL 60204.) The psychologist can and should become involved in these types of preventive activities.

SUMMARY

A multitude of functions, activities, topical areas, and facets of pediatric psychology have been outlined in this chapter. The great variety of these practices provides a challenging and exciting area for research and application. The pediatric psychologist can become involved in an ever changing and growing field for practice and research. The range of activities, rather than any set of procedures or limited conceptualizations, truly illustrates what pediatric psychology is. There is much to be done. The pediatric psychologist innovates, creates, advocates, adapts, applies, and researches to make the field a vibrant one.

Chapter 5

Resources for Pediatric Psychology

This chapter lists available resources for the pediatric psychologist practitioner. This is not an exhaustive compilation, but it does contain the resources for following up information and for networking with other professionals. Psychologists in medical settings and those outside such settings but with interests in pediatric psychology frequently have found these sources useful. These resources include organizations and journals related to pediatric psychology, texts and articles containing material on the range of pediatric and clinical child psychology, literature on assessment of disorders in the field of practice, overview articles and treatment summaries on specific disorders, and basic pediatric medicine textbooks for reference.

ORGANIZATIONS AND JOURNALS

Organizations

Society of Pediatric Psychology (Section 5 of the Division of Clinical Psychology, American Psychological Association). Primary organization for pediatric psychologists and others interested in health psychology for children. Membership includes subscriptions to the *Journal of Pediatric Psychology* (published by Plenum Press) and the *SPP Newsletter.* Contact: J. Kenneth Whitt, PhD, Secretary, Department of Psychiatry, University of North Carolina School of Medicine, Chapel Hill, NC 27514.

Association for the Care of Children's Health. An interdisciplinary group concerned with psychosocial and developmental needs of children and families in health-care settings. Membership includes subscriptions to the journal *Children's Health Care,* and to a newsletter, *ACCH News,* as well as reduced rates for numerous publications and the yearly conference. Contact: ACCH, 3615 Wisconsin Avenue, N.W., Washington, DC 20016.

Society of Behavioral Medicine. An interdisciplinary organization concerned with the integration of behavioral and biomedical sciences with applications in prevention, diagnosis, treatment, and rehabilitation. Membership includes subscriptions to *Annals of Behavioral Medicine* and *Behavioral Medicine Abstracts* (published by Guilford Press) and reduced fees for the annual meeting. Contact: Society of Behavioral Medicine, P.O. Box 8530, University Station, Knoxville, TN 37996.

Division of Health Psychology (Division 38 of the American Psychological Association). A group for psychologists interested in the psychological and behavioral aspects of health. Membership includes subscriptions to *Health Psychology* (published by Lawrence Erlbaum Associates) and a newsletter, *The Health Psychologist.* Programs are sponsored at the annual meeting of the American Psychological Association. Contact: Division 38, American Psychological Association, 1200 Seventeenth Avenue, N.W., Washington, DC 20016.

Society for Behavioral Pediatrics. An interdisciplinary organization, but with more pediatricians than psychologists as members. Goal is to improve children's health care through research and teaching in the areas of developmental and behavioral pediatrics. Central to membership is evidence of scientific inquiry and scholarly activity. SBP holds an annual meeting (in conjunction with Ambulatory Pediatrics Association meetings). Membership includes a subscription to the *Journal of Developmental and Behavioral Pediatrics* (published by Williams & Wilkins). Contact: Ms. Noreen Spota, Business Administrator, SBP, 241 East Gravers Lane, Philadelphia, PA 19118.

Journals

Journal of Pediatric Psychology. Sponsored by Society of Pediatric Psychology (SPP). *JPP* publishes articles related to theory, research, training, and professional practice in pediatric psychology in four issues per year. Subscription is covered in membership fee for SPP. Nonmember individual and institutional subscriptions are available from Plenum Press, 233 Spring Street, New York, NY 10013.

Children's Health Care. Sponsored by Association for the Care of Children's Health (ACCH). *CHC* publishes multidisciplinary articles on research and essays on efforts to foster the psychosocial care of children and families in health-care settings. Subscription is covered in membership fee in ACCH. Nonmember individual and institutional subscriptions are available from ACCH, 3615 Wisconsin Avenue, N.W., Washington, DC 20016.

Journal of Developmental and Behavioral Pediatrics. Sponsored by Society of Behavioral Pediatrics *(SBP).* This journal publishes articles involving the interface between pediatrics, child development, and the behavioral sciences. Membership in SBP includes subscription. Individual subscriptions are available from Williams & Wilkins Company, 428 East Preston Street, Baltimore, MD 21202.

Journal of Clinical Child Psychology. Sponsored by the Section on Clinical Child Psychology of the American Psychological Association. *JCCP* publishes articles on research, practice, and training related to the diverse ways of promoting the well-being of children and youth. Subscription is included in membership fee of section; contact Martha Perry, PhD, Treasurer, 10518 NE 68th Street, Kirkland, WA 98033. Nonmember individual and institutional subscriptions are available from Lawrence Erlbaum Associates, Suite 102, 365 Broadway, Hillsdale, NJ 07642.

Journal of Behavioral Medicine. JBM is an interdisciplinary outlet for articles on research and applications of behavioral science to furthering understanding of physical health and illness. Some articles relate to pediatric topics. Subscriptions are available from Plenum Press, 233 Spring Street, New York, NY 10013.

Pediatrics. This journal is the primary publication in pediatric medicine. It focuses predominantly on diagnosis and treatment of medical disorders with a few articles on psychosocial aspects of pediatric practice. Subscriptions are available from American Academy of Pediatrics, P.O. Box 1034, Evanston, IL 60204.

Child Health Alert. A monthly newsletter for child-care professionals and parents. *CHA* presents and interprets pediatric health information. Summaries of governmental policies and published research are presented and discussed. Subscriptions are available from Child Health Alert, P.O. Box 338, Newton Highlands, MA 02161.

Clinical Pediatrics. This journal is oriented to pediatric practice with behavioral and educational topics included. Published by J.B. Lippincott Company. Subscriptions are available from *Clinical Pediatrics,* 2350 Virginia Avenue, Hagerstown, MD 21740.

A large number of other journals publish articles related to pediatric psychology at least occasionally. These include: *Journal of Consulting and Clinical Psychology, American Journal of Public Health, Developmental Medicine and Child Neurology, Journal of Abnormal Child Psychology, Journal of Autism and Developmental Disorders, Journal of Pediatrics,* and *Journal of Applied Behavior Analysis,* among others. Detailed information on these would be too lengthy to include here. However, additional data on 106 journals publishing articles in child-oriented psychology are available in a compendium of publication outlets (Roberts, Lyman, Breiner, & Royal, 1982).

BOOKS AND ARTICLES

General Pediatric Psychology

Edited Volumes Series

Burns, W. J., & Lavigne, J. V. (Eds.). (1984). *Progress in pediatric psychology.* Orlando, FL: Grune & Stratton.

Fitzgerald, H. E., Lester, B. M., & Yogman, M. W. (Eds.). (1982–1984). *Theory and research in behavioral pediatrics.* (Vols. 1 and 2). New York: Plenum.

Lahey, B. B., & Kazdin, A. E. (Eds.). (1977–1985). *Advances in clinical child psychology* (Vols. 1–8). New York: Plenum.

Wolraich, M., & Routh, D. K. (Eds.). (1981–1985). *Advances in developmental and behavioral pediatrics* (Vols. 1–5). Greenwich, CT: JAI.

Individual Volumes

Firestone, P., McGrath, P. J., & Feldman, W. (Eds.). (1983). *Advances in behavioral medicine for children and adolescents.* Hillsdale, NJ: Lawrence Erlbaum.

Karoly, P., Steffen, J. J., & O'Grady, D. J. (Eds.).(1982). *Child health psychology: Concepts and issues.* New York: Pergamon.

Krasnegor, N. A., Cataldo, M. F., & Arasteh, J. D. (Eds.). (1985). *Child health behavior: Research and priorities in behavioral pediatrics.* New York: Wiley.

Lavigne, J. V., & Burns, W. J. (1981). *Pediatric psychology: An introduction for pediatricians and psychologists.* New York: Grune & Stratton.

Magrab, P. R. (Ed.). (1978). *Psychological management of pediatric problems: Vol. 1. Early life conditions and chronic diseases. Vol. 2. Sensorineural conditions and social concerns.* Baltimore: University Park Press.

Matarazzo, J. D., Weiss, S. M., Herd, J. A., Miller, N. E., & Weiss, S. M. (Eds.). (1984). *Behavioral health: A handbook of health enhancement and disease prevention.* New York: Wiley-Interscience.

McGrath, P. J., & Firestone, P. (Eds.). (1983). *Pediatric and adolescent behavioral medicine.* New York: Springer.

Millon, T., Green, C., & Meagher, R. (Eds.). (1982). *Handbook of clinical health psychology.* New York: Plenum.

Russo, D. C., & Varni, J. W. (Eds.). (1982). *Behavioral pediatrics: Research and practice.* New York: Plenum.

Tuma, J. M. (Ed.). (1982). *Handbook for the practice of pediatric psychology.* New York: Wiley-Interscience.

Varni, J. W. (1983). *Clinical behavioral pediatrics: An interdisciplinary approach.* New York: Pergamon.

Walker, C. E., & Roberts, M. C. (Eds.). (1983). *Handbook of clinical child psychology.* New York: Wiley-Interscience.

Wright, L., Schaefer, A. B., & Solomons, G. (1979). *Encyclopedia of pediatric psychology.* Baltimore: University Park Press.

Assessment in Pediatric Psychology

Karoly, P., & May, C. (Eds.). (in press). *Handbook of child health assessment*. New York: Wiley-Interscience.

Magrab, P. R. (Ed.). (1984). *Psychological and behavioral assessment: Impact on pediatric care*. New York: Plenum.

Mash, E. J., & Terdal, L. G. ʻEds.). (1981). *Behavioral assessment of childhood disorders*. New York: Guilford.

Weaver, S. J. (Ed.). (1984). *Testing children: A reference guide for effective clinical and psychoeducational assessments*. Kansas City, MO: Test Corporation of America.

Basic Pediatric References

Berman, R. E., & Vaughan, V. C., III (Eds.). (1983). *Nelson textbook of pediatrics* (12th ed.). Philadelphia: Saunders.

Kaye, R., Oski, F. A., & Barness, L. A. (Eds.). (1982). *Core textbook of pediatrics* (2nd ed.). Philadelphia: Lippincott.

Levine, M. D., Carey, W. B., Crocker, A. C., & Gross, R. T. (Eds.). (1983). *Developmental-behavioral pediatrics*. Philadelphia: Saunders.

Prugh, D. G. (1983). *The psychosocial aspects of pediatrics*. Philadelphia: Lea & Febiger.

Rudolph, A. M., Hoffman, J. I. E., & Axelrod, S. (Eds.). (1982). *Pediatrics* (7th ed.). Norwalk, CT: Appleton-Century-Crofts.

Shelov, S. P., Mezey, A. P., Edelmann, C. M., Jr., & Barnett, H. L. (Eds.). (1984). *Primary care pediatrics: A symptomatic approach*. Norwalk, CT: Appleton-Century-Crofts.

Selected Specific Disorders

Anorexia Nervosa and Bulimia

Weiss, L., Katzman, M., & Wolchik, S. (1985). *Treating bulimia: A psychoeducational approach*. New York: Pergamon.

Asthma

Creer, T. L., Renne, C. M., & Christian, W. P. (1976). Behavioral contributions to rehabilitation and childhood asthma. *Rehabilitation Literature, 37*, 226–232.

Falliers, C. J. (1983). Asthma, eczema, and related allergies. In M. D. Levine, W. B. Carey, A. C. Crocker, & R. T. Gross (Eds.), *Developmental-behavioral pediatrics* (pp. 474–482). Philadelphia: Saunders.

Anxiety, Fears, & Phobias

Morris, R. J., & Kratochwill, T. R. (1983). *Treating children's fears and phobias*. New York: Pergamon.

Behavioral Noncompliance

Fleischman, M. J., Horne, A. M., & Arthur, J. L. (1983). *Troubled families: A treatment program*. Champaign, IL: Research Press.

Forehand, R. L., & McMahon, R. J. (1981). *Helping the noncompliant child: A clinician's guide to parent training*. New York: Guilford.

Patterson, G. R. (1982). *Coercive family process*. Eugene, OR: Castalia.

Burns

Knudson-Cooper, M. S. (1984). The antecedents and consequences of children's burn injuries. In M. Wolraich & D. K. Routh (Eds.), *Advances in developmental and behavioral pediatrics*. (Vol. 5, pp. 33–74). Greenwich, CT: JAI.

Wisely, D. W., Masur, F. T., & Morgan, S. B. (1983). Psychological aspects of severe burn injuries in children. *Health Psychology, 2,* 45–72.

Childhood Cancer

Kellerman, J. (Ed.). (1980). *Psychological aspects of childhood cancer.* Springfield, IL: Charles C Thomas.

Koocher, G. P., & O'Malley, J. E. (1981). *The Damocles syndrome: Psychosocial consequences of surviving childhood cancer.* New York: McGraw-Hill.

Spinetta, J. J., & Deasy-Spinetta, P. (1981). *Living with childhood cancer.* St. Louis: Mosby.

Childhood Depression

Finch, A. J., & Saylor, C. F. (1984). An overview of child depression. In W. J. Burns & J. V. Lavigne (Eds.), *Progress in pediatric psychology* (pp. 201–239). Orlando, FL: Grune & Stratton.

Childhood Injuries

Baker, S. P. (1984). *The injury fact book.* Lexington, MA: Lexington Books.

Roberts, M. C., Elkins, P. D., & Royal, G. P. (1984). Psychological applications to the prevention of accidents in childhood. In M. C. Roberts & L. Peterson (Eds.), *Prevention of problems in childhood: Psychological research and applications* (pp. 173–199). New York: Wiley-Interscience.

Robertson, L. S. (1983). *Injuries: Causes, control strategies, and public policy.* Lexington, MA: Lexington Books.

Chronic Illness

Blum, R. W. (Ed.). (1984). *Chronic illness and disabilities in childhood and adolescence.* Orlando, FL: Grune & Stratton.

Hobbs, N., & Perrin, J. M. (Eds.). (1985). *Issues in the care of children with chronic illness.* San Francisco: Jossey-Bass.

McCollum, A. T. (1981). *The chronically ill child: A guide for parents and professionals.* New Haven, CT: Yale University Press.

O'Dougherty, M. M. (1983). *Counseling the chronically ill child: Psychological impact and intervention.* Lexington: Lewis.

Death

Jewitt, C. L. (1982). *Helping children cope with separation and loss.* Cambridge, MA: Harvard Common Press.

Rando, T. A. (1984). *Grief, dying, and death.* Champaign, IL: Research Press.

Developmental Disabilities

Harris, S. L. (1983). *Families of the developmentally disabled: A guide to behavioral intervention.* New York: Pergamon.

Lewis, M., & Taft, L. T. (Eds.). (1982). *Developmental disabilities: Theory, assessment, and intervention.* New York: SP Medical & Scientific Books.

Powers, M. D., & Handleman, J. S. (1984). *Behavioral assessment of severe developmental disabilities.* Rockville, MD: Aspen Publications.

Encopresis and Enuresis

Christophersen, E. R., & Rapoff, M. A. (1983). Toileting problems of children. In C. E. Walker & M. C. Roberts (Eds.), *Handbook of clinical child psychology* (pp. 593-615). New York: Wiley-Interscience.

Schaefer, C. E. (1979). *Childhood encopresis and enuresis: Causes and therapy.* New York: Van Nostrand Reinhold.

Wright, L., & Walker, C. E. (1977). Treatment of the child with psychogenic encopresis. *Clinical Pediatrics, 16,* 1042-1045.

Handicaps

Seligman, M. (Ed.). (1983). *The family with a handicapped child: Understanding and treatment.* Orlando, FL: Grune & Stratton.

Hospitalization

Elkins, P. D., & Roberts, M. C. (1983). Psychological preparation for pediatric hospitalization. *Clinical Psychology Review, 3,* 275-295.

Peterson, L., & Brownlee-Duffeck, M. (1984). Prevention of anxiety and pain due to medical and dental procedures. In M. C. Roberts & L. Peterson (Eds.), *Prevention of problems in childhood: Psychological research and applications* (pp. 266-308). New York: Wiley-Interscience.

Siegel, L. J. (1983). Hospitalization and medical care of children. In C. E. Walker & M. C. Roberts (Eds.), *Handbook of clinical child psychology* (pp. 1089-1108). New York: Wiley-Interscience.

Hyperactivity

Barkley, R. A. (1981). *Hyperactive children.* New York: Guilford.

Ross, D. M., & Ross, S. A. (1982). *Hyperactivity: Current issues, research and theory* (2nd ed.). New York: Wiley-Interscience.

Kerasotes, D., & Walker, C. E. (1983). Hyperactive behavior in children. In C. E. Walker & M. C. Roberts (Eds.), *Handbook of clinical child psychology* (pp. 498–523). New York: Wiley-Interscience.

Learning Disabilities
Neeper, R., & Lahey, B. B. (1983). Learning disabilities of children. In C. E. Walker & M. C. Roberts (Eds.), *Handbook of clinical child psychology* (pp. 680–696). New York: Wiley-Interscience.

Medical Noncompliance
Dunbar, J. M., & Stunkard, A. J. (1979). Adherence to diet and drug regimen. In R. Levy, B. Rifland, B. Dennis, & N. Ernest (Eds.), *Nutrition, lipids, and coronary heart disease* (pp. 391–423). New York: Raven.
Jones, J. G. (1983). Compliance with pediatric therapy: A selective review and recommendations. *Clinical Pediatrics, 22,* 262–265.
Varni, J. W., & Wallander, J. L. (1984). Adherence to health-related regimens in chronic disorders. *Clinical Psychology Review, 4,* 585–596.

Mental Retardation
Cleland, C. C. (1983). Mental retardation. In C. E. Walker & M. C. Roberts (Eds.), *Handbook of clinical child psychology* (pp. 640–659). New York: Wiley-Interscience.

Neonatal Intensive Care & Prematurity
Goldberg, S., & DiVitto, B. A. (1983). *Born too soon: Preterm birth and early development.* San Francisco: Freeman.
Gottfried, A. W., & Gaiter, J. L. (Eds.). (1985). *Infant stress under intensive care.* Baltimore: University Park Press.
Holmes, D. L., Reich, J. N., & Pasternak, J. F. (1984). *The development of infants born at risk.* Hillsdale, NJ: Lawrence Erlbaum.

Obesity
LeBow, M. D. (1984). *Child obesity: A new frontier of behavior therapy.* New York: Springer.
Leon, G. R. (1983). *Treating eating disorders: Obesity, anorexia nervosa and bulimia.* Lexington, MA: Lewis.

Pain & Psychogenic Pain
Beales, J. G. (1982). The assessment and management of pain in children. In P. Karoly, J. J. Steffen, & D. J. O'Grady (Eds.), *Child health psychology* (pp. 154–179). New York: Pergamon.
Jeans, M. E. (1983). Pain in children—A neglected area. In P. Firestone, P. J. McGrath, & W. Feldman (Eds.), *Advances in behavioral medicine for children and adolescents* (pp. 23–27). Hillsdale, NJ: Lawrence Erlbaum.

Physical & Sexual Child Abuse

Finkelhor, D., & Browne, A. (1985). The traumatic impact of child sexual abuse: A conceptualization. *American Journal of Orthopsychiatry, 55,* 530–541.

Kelly, J. A. (1983). *Treating child-abusive families: Interventions based on skills training principles.* New York: Plenum.

Wolfe, D. A. (1985). Child-abusive parents: An empirical review and analysis. *Psychological Bulletin, 97,* 462–482.

Prevention & Health Promotion

Coates, T., Peterson, A., & Perry, C. (Eds.). (1982). *Promoting adolescent health: A dialogue on research and practice.* New York: Academic Press.

Felner, R. D., Jason, L. A., Moritsugu, J. N., & Farber, S. S. (Eds.). (1983). *Preventive psychology: Theory, research, and practice.* New York: Pergamon.

Matarazzo, J. D., Miller, N. E., Weiss, S. M., Herd, J. A., & Weiss, S. M. (Eds.). (1984). *Behavioral health: A handbook of health enhancement and disease prevention.* New York: Wiley-Interscience.

Roberts, M. C., & Peterson, L. (Eds.). *Prevention of problems in childhood: Psychological research and applications.* Wiley-Interscience.

References

Abikoff, H., Gittleman-Klein, K., & Klein, D. J. (1977). Validation of a classroom observation code for hyperactive children. *Journal of Consulting and Clinical Psychology, 45*, 772-783.

Achenbach, T. M. (1978). The child behavior profile: I. Boys aged 6-11. *Journal of Consulting and Clinical Psychology, 46*, 478-488.

Achenbach T. M. (1982). *Developmental psychopathology* (2nd ed.). New York: Wiley.

Adams, B. (1979). *Like it is: Facts and feelings about handicaps from kids who know.* New York: Walker.

Adams, D. W., & Deveau, E. J. (1984). *Coping with childhood cancer: Where do we go from here?* Reston, VA: Reston.

Allen, C. M., & Shinefield, H. R. (1974). Automated multiphasic screening. *Pediatrics, 54*, 611-626.

Als, H., Lester, B. M., Tronick, E. Z., & Brazelton, T. B. (1982). Toward a research instrument for the assessment of preterm infants' behavior (APIB). In H. E. Fitzgerald, B. M. Lester, & M. W. Yogman (Eds.), *Theory and research in behavioral pediatrics* (Vol. 1, pp. 35-132). New York: Plenum.

American Medical Association. (1976). *Distribution of physicians in the United States, 1965-1976.* Chicago: Author.

American Medical Association. (1977). *Profile of medical practice.* Chicago: AMA Center for Health Services Research and Development.

American Psychiatric Association. (1980). *Diagnostic and statistical manual of mental disorders* (3rd ed.). Washington, D.C.: Author.

Anderson, H.W., & Anderson, G. S. (1981). *Mom and dad are divorced but I'm not: Parenting after divorce.* Chicago: Nelson-Hall.

Aradine, C. R. (1976). Books for children about death. *Pediatrics, 57*, 372-378.

Asken, M. J. (1975). Medical psychology: Psychology's neglected child. *Professional Psychology, 6*, 155-160.

Association for the Care of Children's Health. (1985). *ACCH Annotated Media Bibliography.* Washington, DC: Author.

Athreya, B. H. (1980). *Clinical methods in pediatric diagnosis.* New York: Van Nostrand.

Atkeson, B. M., & Forehand, R. (1981). Conduct disorders. In E. J. Mash & L. G. Terdal (Eds.), *Behavioral assessment of childhood disorders* (pp. 185-219). New York: Guilford.

Azrin, N. H., & Besalel, V. A. (1979). *A parent's guide to bedwetting control: A step-by-step method.* New York: Simon & Schuster.

Azrin, N. H., & Foxx, R. M. (1974). *Toilet training in less than a day.* New York: Simon & Schuster.

Azrin, N. H., Sneed, T. J., & Foxx, R. M. (1974). Dry-bed training: Rapid elimination of childhood enuresis. *Behaviour Research and Therapy, 12,* 147–156.

Barkley, R. A. (1981). Hyperactivity. In E. J. Mash & L. G. Terdal (Eds.), *Behavioral assessment of childhood disorders* (pp. 127–184). New York: Guilford.

Barnard, J. D., Christophersen, E. R., & Wolf, M. M. (1977). Teaching children appropriate shopping behavior through parent training in the supermarket setting. *Journal of Applied Behavior Analysis, 10,* 49–59.

Barrios, B. A., Hartmann, D. P., & Shigetomi, C. (1981). Fears and anxieties in children. In E. J. Mash & L. G. Terdal (Eds.), *Behavioral assessment of childhood disorders* (pp. 259–304). New York: Guilford.

Bayley, N. (1969). *Bayley Scales of Infant Development: Birth to two years.* New York: Psychological Corporation.

Becker, J. V., Turner, S. M., & Sajwaj, T. E. (1978). Multiple behavioral effects of the use of lemon juice with a ruminating toddler-age child. *Behavior Modification, 2,* 267–278.

Becker, W. C. (1971). *Parents are teachers.* Champaign, IL: Research Press.

Bergman, A. B. (1986). The business of missing children. *Pediatrics, 77,* 119–121.

Bergman, A. B., Dassel, S. W., & Wedgewood, R.J. (1966). Time-motion study of practicing pediatricians. *Pediatrics, 38,* 254–263.

Bernstein, J. E., & Gullo, S. V.(1977). *When people die.* New York: Dutton.

Bernstein, N. R., Sanger, S., & Fras, J. (1969). The functions of the child psychiatrist in the management of severely burned children. *Journal of the American Academy of Child Psychiatry, 8,* 620–635.

Bibace, R., & Walsh, N. E. (1980). Development of children's concepts of illness. *Pediatrics, 66,* 912–917.

Blount, R. L., Dahlquist, L. M., Baer, R. A., & Wuori, D. (1984). A brief, effective method for teaching children to swallow pills. *Behavior Therapy, 15,* 381–387.

Blume, J. (1972). *It's not the end of the world.* Scarsdale, NY: Bradbury.

Bonsall, C. (1980). *Who's afraid of the dark?.* New York: Harper & Row.

Brazelton, T. B. (1975). Anticipatory guidance. In S. B. Friedman (Ed.), *The pediatric clinics of North America* (pp. 533–544). Philadelphia: Saunders.

Brazelton, T. B. (1984). *The Neonatal Behavioral Assessment Scale* (2nd ed.). (Clinics in Developmental Medicine, no. 88). Philadelphia: Lippincott.

Brewer, D. (1978). The role of the psychologist in a dialysis and transplantation unit. *Journal of Clinical Child Psychology, 7,* 71–72.

Bronheim, S. M., & Jacobstein, D. M. (1984). Psychosocial assessment in chronic and fatal illness. In P. R. Magrab (Ed.), *Psychological and behavioral assessment: Impact on pediatric care* (pp. 279–335). New York: Plenum.

Brooks, R. B. (1983). *So that's how I was born!* New York: Little Simon.

Brown, M. W. (1958). *The dead bird.* New York: Young Scott.

Burnett, R. D., & Bell, L. S. (1978). Projecting pediatric practice patterns: Report of the survey of the Pediatric Manpower Committee. *Pediatrics, 62* (4, Pt. 2), 625–680.

Burnett, R. D., Williams, M. K., & Olmsted, R. W. (1978). Pediatrics manpower requirements. *Pediatrics, 61,* 438–445.

Burns, B.J., & Cromer, W. W. (1978). The evolving role of the psychologist in primary health care practitioner training for mental health services. *Journal of Clinical Child Psychology, 7,* 8–12.

Butler, J. F. (1976). The toilet training success of parents after reading *Toilet Training in Less Than a Day. Behavior Therapy, 7,* 185–191.

Cameron, J. R., & Rice, D. C. (1986). Developing anticipatory guidance programs based on early assessment of infant temperament: Two tests of a prevention model. *Journal of Pediatric Psychology, 11,* 221–234.

Campbell, S. B. (1983). Developmental perspectives in child psychopathology. In T. H. Ollendick &

M. Hersen (Eds.), *Handbook of child psychotherapy* (pp. 13–40). New York: Plenum.

Cataldo, M. F., Bessman, C. A., Parker, L. H., Pearson, J. E. R., & Rogers, M. C. (1979). Behavioral assessment for pediatric intensive care units. *Journal of Applied Behavior Analysis, 12,* 83–97.

Cautela, J., & Brion-Meisels, L. A. (1979). Children's reinforcement survey schedule. *Psychological Reports, 44,* 327–338.

Christophersen, E. R. (1977). *Little people: Guidelines for common sense child-rearing.* Lawrence, KS: H & H Enterprises.

Christophersen, E. R. (1982). Incorporating behavioral pediatrics into primary care. In E. R. Christophersen (Ed.), *Symposium on Behavioral Pediatrics: Pediatric Clinics of North America, 29* (2), 261–296.

Christophersen, E. R., & Barnard, J. D. (1978). Management of behavior problems: A perspective for pediatricians. *Clinical Pediatrics, 17,* 122–124.

Christophersen, E. R., & Gyulay, J. E. (1981). Parental compliance with car seat usage: A positive approach with long-term follow-up. *Journal of Pediatric Psychology, 6,* 301–312.

Christophersen, E. R., & Rainey, S. K. (1976). Management of encopresis through a pediatric outpatient clinic. *Journal of Pediatric Psychology, 1,* 38–41.

Christophersen, E. R., & Rapoff, M. A. (1980). Pediatric psychology: An appraisal. In B. B. Lahey & A. E. Kazdin (Eds.), *Advances in clinical child psychology* (Vol. 3, pp. 311–332). New York: Plenum.

Christophersen, E. R., & Rapoff, M. A. (1983). Toileting problems of children. In C. E. Walker & M. C. Roberts (Eds.), *Handbook of clinical child psychology* (pp. 593–615). New York: Wiley-Interscience.

Christophersen, E. R., Sosland-Edelman, D., & LeClaire, S. (1985). An evaluation of two comprehensive infant car seat loaner programs with one year follow-up. *Pediatrics, 76,* 36–42.

Cilotta, C., & Livingston, C. (1981). *Why am I going to the hospital?* Secaucus, NJ: Lyle Stuart.

Cleland, C. I. (1983). Mental retardation. In C. E. Walker & M. C. Roberts (Eds.), *Handbook of clinical child psychology* (pp. 640–659). New York: Wiley-Interscience.

Conners, C. K. (1969). A teacher rating scale for use in doing studies with children. *American Journal of Psychiatry, 126,* 884–888.

Creer, T. L., Renne, C. M., & Christian, W. P. (1976). Behavioral contributions to rehabilitation and childhood asthma. *Rehabilitation Literature, 37,* 226–232.

Davis, P. K., & Cuvo, A. J. (1980). Chronic vomiting and rumination in intellectually normal and retarded individuals: Review and evaluation of behavioral research. *Behavior Research of Severe Developmental Disabilities, 1,* 31–59.

Dawson, G., & Mesibov, G. B. (1983). Childhood psychoses. In C. E. Walker & M. C. Roberts (Eds.), *Handbook of clinical child psychology* (pp. 543–572). New York: Wiley-Interscience.

Dershewitz, R. A., & Christophersen, E. R. (1984). Childhood household safety: An overview. *American Journal of Diseases of Childhood, 138,* 85–88.

Division of Health Psychology: American Psychological Association. (undated). *Health psychology: New perspectives.* Washington, DC: Author.

Drabman, R. S., & Jarvie, G. (1977). Counseling parents of children with behavior problems: The use of extinction and time-out techniques. *Pediatrics, 59,* 78–85.

Drabman, R. S., & Rosenbaum, M. S. (1980). Pediatric counseling with parents regarding childhood behavior problems: Misbehavior away from home and early morning dawdlers. *Journal of Developmental and Behavioral Pediatrics, 1,* 86–88.

Drotar, D. (1977). Clinical psychological practice in a pediatric hospital. *Professional Psychology, 7,* 72–80.

Drotar, D. (1978). Training psychologists to consult with pediatricians: Problems and prospects. *Journal of Clinical Child Psychology, 7,* 57–60.

Drotar, D. (1982). The child psychologist in the medical system. In P. Karoly, J. J. Steffen, & D. J.

O'Grady (Eds.), *Child health psychology* (pp. 1–28). New York: Pergamon.

Drotar, D., Benjamin, P., Chwast, R., Litt, C., & Vajner, P. (1982). The role of the psychologist in pediatric outpatient and inpatient settings. In J. M. Tuma (Ed.), *Handbook for the practice of pediatric psychology* (pp. 228–250). New York: Wiley-Interscience.

Drotar, D., Crawford, P., & Ganofsky, M. A. (1984). Prevention with chronically ill children. In M. C. Roberts & L. Peterson (Eds.), *Prevention of problems in childhood: Psychological research and applications* (pp. 232–265). New York: Wiley-Interscience.

Drotar, D., Doershuk, C. F., Stern, R. C., Boat, T. F., Boyer, W., & Matthews, L. (1981). Psychosocial functioning of children with cystic fibrosis. *Pediatrics, 67,* 338–343.

Duff, R. S., Rowe, D. S., & Anderson, F. P. (1973). Patient care and student learning in a pediatric clinic. *Pediatrics, 50,* 839–846.

Elkins, P. D., & Roberts, M. C. (1983). Psychological preparation for pediatric hospitalization. *Clinical Psychology Review, 3,* 275–295.

Elkins, P. D., & Roberts, M. C. (1984). A preliminary evaluation of hospital preparation for nonpatient children: Primary prevention in a "let's pretend hospital." *Children's Health Care, 13,* 31–36.

Elkins, P. D., & Roberts, M. C. (1985). Reducing medical fears in a general population of children: A comparison of three audiovisual modeling procedures. *Journal of Pediatric Psychology, 10,* 65–75.

Elliott, C. H., & Olson, R. A. (1982). Variations in conditioning procedures for the decannulation of tracheostomy-dependent children: Clinical and theoretical implications. *Health Psychology, 1,* 389–397.

Eyberg, S. M., & Matarazzo, R. G. (1980). Training parents as therapists: A comparison between individual parent–child interaction training and parent group didactic training. *Journal of Clinical Psychology, 36,* 492–499.

Falliers, C. J. (1983). Asthma, eczema, and related allergies. In M. D. Levine, W. B. Carey, A. C. Crocker, & R. T. Gross (Eds.), *Developmental-behavioral pediatrics* (pp. 474–482). Philadelphia: Saunders.

Fassler, J. (1969). *One little girl.* New York: Human Sciences Press.

Fassler, J. (1972). *The boy with a problem: Johnny learns to share his troubles.* New York: Human Sciences Press.

Fassler, J. (1975). *Howie helps himself.* New York: Albert Whitman.

Feldman, G. (1976). The effect of biofeedback training on respiratory resistance of asthmatic children. *Psychosomatic Medicine, 38,* 27–34.

Fordyce, W. E. (1976). *Behavioral methods for chronic pain and illness.* St. Louis: Mosby.

Forehand, R. L., & McMahon, R. J. (1981). *Helping the noncompliant child: A clinician's guide to parent training.* New York: Guilford.

Forgatch, M. S., & Toobert, D. J. (1979). A cost-effective parent training program for use with normal preschool children. *Journal of Pediatric Psychology, 4,* 129–145.

Frankenburg, W. K., Fandal, A. W., Sciarillo, W., & Burgess, D. (1981). The newly abbreviated and revised Denver Developmental Screening Test. *Journal of Pediatrics, 99,* 995–999.

Friedman, R. M., Sandler, S., Hernandez, M., & Wolfe, D. A. (1981). Child abuse. In E. J. Mash & L. G. Terdal (Eds.), *Behavioral assessment of childhood disorders* (pp. 221–255). New York: Guilford.

Funk, M. J., Mullins, L. L., & Olson, R. A. (1984). Teaching children to swallow pills: A case study. *Children's Health Care, 13,* 20–23.

Gardner, R. A. (1970). *The boys and girls book about divorce.* New York: Bantam.

Gayton, W., Friedman, S., Tavormina, J., & Tucker, F. (1977). Children with cystic fibrosis: Psychological test findings of patients, siblings, and parents. *Pediatrics, 59,* 888–894.

Geist, R. A. (1977). Consultation on a pediatric surgical ward: Creating an empathic climate. *American Journal of Orthopsychiatry, 47,* 432–444.

Glennon, B., & Weisz, J. R. (1978). An observational approach to the assessment of anxiety in young children. *Journal of Consulting and Clinical Psychology, 46*, 1246-1257.

Gordon, S. (1983). *Girls are girls and boys are boys, so what's the difference?* Fayetteville, NY: Ed-U Press.

Gordon, S., & Gordon, J. (1983). *Raising a child conservatively in a sexually permissive world.* New York: Simon and Schuster.

Gottfried, A. W., Guerin, D., Spencer, J. E., & Meyer, C. (1984). Validity of Minnesota Child Development Inventory in screening young children's developmental status. *Journal of Pediatric Psychology, 9*, 219-230.

Gottlieb, M. I. (1983). Otitis media. In M. D. Levine, W. B. Carey, A. C. Crocker, & R. T. Gross (Eds.), *Developmental-behavioral pediatrics* (pp. 463-473). Philadelphia: Saunders.

Green, M. (1980). The pediatric model of care. *Behavioral Medicine Update, 2*(4), 11-13.

Green, M. (1983). Sources of pain. In M. D. Levine, W. B. Carey, A. C. Crocker, & R. T. Gross (Eds.), *Developmental-behavioral pediatrics* (pp. 512-518). Philadelphia: Saunders.

Gross, A. M., Eudy, C., & Drabman, R. S. (1982). Training parents to be physical therapists with their physically handicapped child. *Journal of Behavioral Medicine, 5*, 321-327.

Grossman, C. S. (1983a). Children's books: A child's view of death. *Clinical Pediatrics, 22*, 70-71.

Grossman, C. S. (1983b). Children's books: Coping with divorce. *Clinical Pediatrics, 22*, 230-231.

Grossman, C. S. (1983c). Children's books: Keeping lines of communication open between parents and their adopted children. *Clinical Pediatrics, 22*, 526.

Grossman, C. S. (1983d). Children's books: Educating about alcoholism. *Clinical Pediatrics, 22*, 719-720.

Grossman, C. S. (1984a). Children's books: Reducing a child's fear of medical treatments. *Clinical Pediatrics, 23*, 114-115.

Grossman, C. S. (1984b). Children's books: Developing positive attitudes by and toward the handicapped. *Clinical Pediatrics, 23*, 448-463.

Grossman, C. S. (1984c). Children's books: Answering children's questions about where babies come from. *Clinical Pediatrics, 23*, 661-662.

Grossman, C. S. (1985). Children's books: Dealing with prolonged illness. *Clinical Pediatrics, 24*, 110-111.

Gruenberg, S. M. (1970). *The wonderful story of how you were born.* New York: Doubleday.

Harper, R. G. (1975). Behavior modification in pediatric practice. *Clinical Pediatrics, 14*, 962-967.

Harries, J. (1981). *They triumphed over their handicaps.* New York: Franklin Watts.

Harris, S. L., & Ferrari, M. (1983). Developmental factors in child behavior therapy. *Behavior Therapy, 14*, 54-72.

Hartlage, L. C., & Hartlage, P. L. (1978). Clinical consultation to pediatric neurology and developmental pediatrics. *Journal of Clinical Child Psychology, 7*, 19-20.

Hayes, M. L. (1974). *The tuned-in, turned-on book about learning problems.* Novato, CA: Academic Therapy Publications.

Hazen, B. S. (1983). *Two homes to live in. A child's eye view of divorce.* New York: Human Sciences Press.

Hermes, P. (1980). *What if they knew?* New York: Harcourt, Brace, & Jovanovich.

Hetherington, E. M., Cox, M., & Cox, R. (1979). Play and social interaction in children following divorce. *Journal of Social Issues, 35*, 26-49.

Hilgard, J., & LeBaron, S. (1982). Relief of anxiety and pain in children with cancer: Quantitative measures and qualitative clinical observations in a flexible approach. *International Journal of Clinical and Experimental Hypnosis, 30*, 417-441.

Hillman, H. S., Jones, R. T., & Farmer, L. (1986). The acquisition and maintenance of fire emergency skills: Effects of rationale and behavioral practice. *Journal of Pediatric Psychology, 11*, 247-258.

Hirsch, D. L. O., & Russo, D. C. (1983) Behavior management. In M. D. Levine, W. B. Carey, A. C. Crocker, & R. T. Gross (Eds.), *Developmental-behavioral pediatrics* (pp. 1068-1099). Philadelphia: Saunders.

Hodges, K., Kline, J., Fitch, P., McKnew, D., & Cytryn, L. (1981). The child assessment schedule: A diagnostic interview for research and clinical use. *Catalog of Selected Documents in Psychology, 11,* 56.

Hodges, K., Kline, J., Stern, L., Cytryn, L., & McKnew, D. (1982). The development of a child assessment interview for research and clinical use. *Journal of Abnormal Child Psychology, 10,* 173-189.

Howe, J. (1981). *The hospital book.* New York: Crown.

Ingersoll, B., & Curry, F. (1977). Rapid treatment of persistent vomiting in a 14-year-old female by shaping and time-out. *Journal of Behavior Therapy and Experimental Psychiatry, 8,* 305-307.

Ireton, H., & Thwing, E. (1974). *Minnesota Child Development Inventory.* Minneapolis, MN: Behavior Science Systems.

Jay, S. M., Ozolins, M., Elliott, C. H., & Caldwell, S. (1983). Assessment of children's distress during painful medical procedures. *Health Psychology, 2,* 133-147.

Jones, C. R. (1981). *Angie and me.* New York: Macmillan.

Jones, J. G. (1983). Compliance with pediatric therapy. *Clinical Pediatrics, 22,* 262-265.

Jones, R. T., Kazdin, A. E., & Haney, J. I. (1981a). A follow-up to training emergency skills. *Behavior Therapy, 12,* 716-722.

Jones, R. T., Kazdin, A. E., & Haney, J. I. (1981b). Social validation and training of emergency fire safety skills for potential injury prevention and life saving. *Journal of Applied Behavior Analysis, 14,* 249-260.

Kagan, J. (1965). The new marriage: Pediatrics and psychology. *American Journal of Diseases of Childhood, 110,* 272-278.

Kanoy, K. W., & Schroeder, C. S. (1985). Suggestions to parents about common behavior problems in a pediatric primary care office: Five years of follow-up. *Journal of Pediatric Psychology, 10,* 15-30.

Karoly, P., & May, C. (Eds.). (in press). *Handbook of child health assessment: Biopsychosocial perspectives.* New York: Wiley.

Karoly, P., Steffen, J. J., & O'Grady, D. J. (Eds.). (1982). *Child health psychology.* New York: Pergamon.

Katz, K. S. (1984). Attention deficit and learning disorders. In P. Magrab (Ed.), *Psychological and behavioral assessment* (pp. 191-233). New York: Plenum.

Kellerman, J. (Ed.). (1980). *Psychological aspects of cancer in children.* Springfield, IL: Charles C Thomas.

Kelley, M. L., Jarvie, G. J., Middlebrook, J. L., McNeer, M. F., & Drabman, R. S. (1984). Decreasing burned children's pain behavior: Impacting the trauma of hydrotherapy. *Journal of Applied Behavior Analysis, 17,* 147-158.

Kenny, T. J., Bergey, S. F. A., & Young-Hyman, D. (1983). Psychosomatic problems of children. In C. E. Walker & M. C. Roberts (Eds.), *Handbook of clinical child psychology* (pp. 437-452). New York: Wiley-Interscience.

Klinzing, D. R., & Klinzing, D. G. (1977). Communicating with young children about hospitalization. *Communication Education, 26,* 307-313.

Knitzer, J. (1982). *Unclaimed children.* Washington, DC: Children's Defense Fund.

Koeppen, A. S. (1974). Relaxation training for children. *Elementary School Guidance and Counseling, 9,* 14-21.

Kolko, D. J., & Rickard-Figueroa, J. L. (1985). Effects of video games on the adverse corollaries of chemotherapy in pediatric oncology patients: A single-case analysis. *Journal of Consulting and Clinical Psychology, 53,* 223-238.

Koocher, G. P., & Berman, S. J. (1983). Life threatening and terminal illness in childhood. In M. D. Levine, W. B.Carey, A. C. Crocker, & R. T. Gross (Eds.), *Developmental-behavioral pediatrics* (pp. 488-501). Philadelphia: Saunders.

Koocher, G. P., & Sallan, S. E. (1978). Pediatric oncology. In P. R. Magrab (Ed.), *Psychological management of pediatric problems: Vol. 1. Early life conditions and chronic diseases* (pp. 283-307). Baltimore: University Park Press.

Koocher, G. P., Sourkes, B.M., & Keane, W. M. (1979). Pediatric oncology consultations: A generalizable model for medical settings. *Professional Psychology, 10,* 467-474.

Krementz, J. (1981). *How it feels when a parent dies.* New York: Knopf.

Kucia, C., Drotar, D., Doershuk, C. F., Stern, R. C., Boat, T. F.,& Matthews, L. (1979). Home observation of family interaction and childhood adjustment to cystic fibrosis. *Journal of Pediatric Psychology, 4,* 189-195.

La Greca, A. M., & Ottinger, D. R. (1979). Self-monitoring and relaxation training in the treatment of medically ordered exercises in a 12-year-old female. *Journal of Pediatric Psychology, 4,* 49-54.

La Greca, A. M., & Stone, W. L. (1985). Behavioral pediatrics. In N. Schneiderman & J. Tapp (Eds.), *Behavioral pediatrics: The biopsychosocial approach* (pp. 255-291). Hillsdale, NJ: Lawrence Erlbaum.

Lavigne, J. V., & Burns, W. J. (1981). *Pediatric psychology: An introduction for pediatricians.* New York: Grune & Stratton.

Levine, E. S. (1974). *Lisa and her soundless world.* New York: Human Sciences Press.

Levine, M. D., Carey, W. B., Crocker, A. C., & Gross, R. T. (Eds.). (1983). *Developmental-behavioral pediatrics.* Philadelphia: Saunders.

Levy, R. L., Lodish, D., & Pawlak-Floyd, C. (1982). Teaching children to take more responsibility for their own dental treatment. *Social Work in Health Care, 7,* 69-76.

Lewis, S. (1978). Considerations in setting up psychological consultation to a pediatric hematology-oncology team. *Journal of Clinical Child Psychology, 7,* 21-22.

Lichtenstein, R., & Ireton, H. (1984). *Preschool screening.* Orlando, FL: Grune & Stratton.

Liebman, R., Minuchin, S., & Baker, L. (1974). The use of structural family therapy in the treatment of intractable asthma. *American Journal of Psychiatry, 131,* 535-540.

Linscheid, T. R. (1978). Disturbances of eating and feeding. In P. R. Magrab (Ed.), *Psychological management of pediatric problems: Vol. 1. Early life conditions and chronic diseases* (pp. 191-218). Baltimore: University Park Press.

Linscheid, T. R. (1983). Eating problems in childhood. In C. E. Walker & M. C. Roberts (Eds.), *Handbook of clinical child psychology* (pp. 616-639). New York: Wiley-Interscience.

Linscheid, T. R.,& Cunningham, C. E. (1977). A controlled demonstration of the effectiveness of electric shock in the elimination of chronic infant rumination. *Journal of Applied Behavior Analysis, 10,* 500.

Lowe, K., & Lutzker, J. R. (1979). Increasing compliance to a medical regimen with a juvenile diabetic. *Behavior Therapy, 10,* 57-64.

Lynch, M. (1979). *Mary Fran and Mo.* New York: St. Martin's Press.

Lyman, R. D., & Roberts, M. C. (1984). Assessment of children with psychosomatic disorders. In S. J. Weaver (Ed.), *Testing children: A reference guide for effective clinical and psychoeducational assessments* (pp. 37-49). Kansas City, MO: Test Corporation of America.

Lyman, R. D., & Roberts, M. C. (1985). Mental health testimony in child custody litigation. *Law and Psychology Review, 9,* 15-34.

MacPhee, D. (1984). The pediatrician as a source of information about child development. *Journal of Pediatric Psychology, 9,* 87-100.

Madden, N. A., Russo, D. C., & Cataldo, M. F. (1980a). Behavioral treatment of pica in children with lead poisoning. *Child Behavior Therapy, 2,* 67-81.

Madden, N. A., Russo, D. C., & Cataldo, M. F. (1980b). Environmental influences in mouthing in children with lead intoxication. *Journal of Pediatric Psychology, 5,* 207-216.

Maddux, J. E., Roberts, M. C., Sledden, E. A., & Wright, L. (1986). Developmental issues in child health psychology. *American Psychologist, 41,* 25-34.

Magid, K., & Schreibman, W. (1980). *Divorce is . . . a kid's coloring book.* Gretna, LA: Pelican.

Magrab, P. R. (1984a). A developmental framework for psychological assessment of pediatric conditions. In P. R. Magrab (Ed.), *Psychological and behavioral assessment* (pp. 3-21). New York: Plenum.

Magrab, P. R. (Ed.). (1984b). *Psychological and behavioral assessment.* New York: Plenum.

Magrab, P. R., & Papadopoulou, Z. (1977). The effect of a token economy on dietary compliance for children on hemodialysis. *Journal of Applied Behavior Analysis, 10,* 573-579.

Mash, E. J., & Terdal, L. G. (Eds.). (1981). *Behavioral assessment of childhood disorders.* New York: Guilford.

Masur, F. T. (1979). An update on medical psychology and behavioral medicine. *Professional Psychology, 10,* 259-264.

Matarazzo, J. D. (1980). Behavioral health and behavioral medicine: Frontiers for a new health psychology. *American Psychologist, 35,* 807-817.

Matarazzo, J. D. (1984). Behavioral health: A 1990 challenge for the health sciences professions. In J. D. Matarazzo, S. M. Weiss, J. A. Herd, N. E. Miller, & S. M. Weiss (Eds.), *Behavioral health: A handbook of health enhancement and disease prevention* (pp. 3-40). New York: Wiley-Interscience.

Matson, J. L., & Ollendick, T. H. (1977). Issues in toilet training normal children. *Behavior Therapy, 8,* 549-553.

McClelland, C. Q., Staples, W. P., Weisberg, I., & Berger, M. E. (1973). The practitioners' role in behavioral pediatrics. *Journal of Pediatrics, 82,* 325-331.

McGrath, P. J. (1983). Psychological aspects of recurrent abdominal pain. *Canadian Family Physician, 29,* 1655-1659.

McGrath, P. J., Dunn-Geier, J., Cunningham, S. J., Brunette, R., D'Astous, J., Humphreys, P., Latter, J., & Keene, D. (1985). Psychological guidelines for helping children cope with chronic benign intractable pain. *The Clinical Journal of Pain, 1*(3), 1-5.

McGrath, P. J., Johnson, G., Goodman, J. T., Schillinger, J., Dunn, J., & Chapman, J. (1985). CHEOPS: A behavioral scale for rating postoperative pain in children. In H. L. Fields (Ed.), *Advances in pain research and therapy* (Vol. 9, pp. 395-402). New York: Raven.

Melamed, B.G., & Siegel, L. J. (1975). Reduction of anxiety in children facing hospitalization and surgery by use of modeling. *Journal of Consulting and Clinical Psychology, 43,* 511-521.

Mesibov, G. B., Schroeder, C. S., & Wesson, L. (1977). Parental concerns about their children. *Journal of Pediatric Psychology, 2,* 13-17.

Metz, J. R., Allen, C. M., Barr, G., & Shinefield, H. R. (1976). A pediatric screening examination for psychosocial problems. *Pediatrics, 58,* 595-606.

Miller, A. J., & Kratochwill, T. R. (1979). Reduction of frequent stomach complaints by time out. *Behavior Therapy, 10,* 211-218.

Morgan, J. R., & Cullen, P. M. (1980, March). *Giving (almost) psychology away: A multi-level preventive program for providing child rearing advice to parents of pre-schoolers.* Paper presented at the convention of the Southeastern Psychological Association, Washington, DC.

Morgan, S. B. (1984). Helping parents understand the diagnosis of autism. *Journal of Developmental and Behavioral Pediatrics, 5,* 78-85.

Morgan, W. L., & Engel, G. L. (1969). *The clinical approach to the patient.* Philadelphia: Saunders.

Munford, P. R., & Pally, R. (1979). Outpatient contingency management of operant vomiting. *Journal of Behavior Therapy and Experimental Psychiatry, 10,* 135-137.

Murray, J. A., & Epstein, L. H. (1981). Improving oral hygiene with videotape modeling. *Behavior Modification, 5,* 360-371.

National Center for Health Statistics Growth Charts. (1976). *Monthly Vital Statistics Report* (Vol. 25, No. 3, HRA No. 76-1120). Rockville, MD: Health Resources Administration.

Nelson, W. E., Vaughan, V. C., & McKay, R. J. (1975). *Textbook of pediatrics*. Philadelphia: Saunders.

Newcomb, A. F., Chenkin, C. G., Card, A. L., & Ialongo, N. S. (1984). Parentline: A demonstration program for graduate practicum training and community service in clinical child psychology. *Professional Psychology, 15*, 75-81.

Osman, B. B. (1982). *No one to play with: The social side of learning disabilities*. New York: Random House.

Ottinger, D. R., & Roberts, M. C. (1980). A university-based predoctoral practicum in pediatric psychology. *Professional Psychology, 11*, 707-713.

Patterson, G. R. (1982). *Coercive family process*. Eugene, OR: Castalia.

Patterson, G. R., & Gullion, M. E. (1968). *Living with children: New methods for parents and teachers*. Champaign, IL: Research Press.

Perlman, J. L., & Routh, D. K. (1980). Stigmatizing effects of a child's wheelchair in successive and simultaneous interactions. *Journal of Pediatric Psychology, 5*, 43-55.

Peterson, L. (1984a). Book review of Shield, R. R., *Making babies in the 80's: Common sense for new parents. Journal of Pediatric Psychology, 9*, 274-276.

Peterson, L. (1984b). The "Safe-at-Home" game: Training comprehensive safety skills to latch-key children. *Behavior Modification, 18*, 474-494.

Peterson, L. (1984c). Teaching home safety and survival skills to latch-key children: A comparison of two manuals and methods. *Journal of Applied Behavior Analysis, 17*, 279-293.

Peterson, L., & Brownlee-Duffeck, M. (1984). Prevention of anxiety and pain due to medical and dental procedures. In M. C. Roberts & L. Peterson (Eds.), *Prevention of problems in childhood: Psychological research and applications* (pp. 266-308). New York: Wiley-Interscience.

Peterson, L., Mori, L., & Scissors, C. (1986). Mom or dad says I shouldn't: Supervised and unsupervised children's knowledge of their parents' rules for home safety. *Journal of Pediatric Psychology, 11*, 177-188.

Peterson, L., & Roberts, M. C. (in press). Community intervention and prevention. In H. C. Quay & J. S. Werry (Eds.), *Psychopathological disorders of childhood* (3rd ed.). New York: Wiley.

Petrie, P. A., Kratochwill, T. R., Bergan, J. R., & Nicholson, G. I. (1981). Teaching parents to teach their children: Applications in the pediatric setting. *Journal of Pediatric Psychology, 6*, 275-292.

Phillips, D., Fischer, S. G., & Singh, R. (1977). A children's reinforcement survey schedule. *Journal of Behavior Therapy and Experimental Psychiatry, 8*, 131-134.

Poche, C., Brouwer, R., & Swearingen, M. (1981). Teaching self-protection to young children. *Journal of Applied Behavior Analysis, 14*, 169-176.

Potter, P. C., & Roberts, M. C. (1984). Children's perceptions of chronic illness: The roles of disease symptoms, cognitive development, and information. *Journal of Pediatric Psychology, 9*, 13-27.

Prugh, D. G. (1983). *The psychosocial aspects of pediatrics*. Philadelphia: Lea & Febiger.

Rainey, S. K., & Christophersen, E. R. (1976). Behavioral pediatrics: The role of the nurse clinician. *Comprehensive Issues in Pediatric Nursing, 1*, 19-28.

Rapoff, M. A., Christophersen, E. R., & Rapoff, K. E. (1982). The management of common childhood bedtime problems by pediatric nurse practitioners. *Journal of Pediatric Psychology, 7*, 179-196.

Renne, C. M., & Creer, T. L. (1976). Training children with asthma to use inhalation therapy equipment. *Journal of Applied Behavior Analysis, 9*, 1-11.

Rheingold, H. L. (1945). Interpreting mental retardation to parents. *Journal of Consulting Psychology, 9*, 142-148.

Richardson, G. M., McGrath, P. J., Cunningham, S. J., & Humphreys, P. (1983). Validity of the headache diary for children. *Headache, 23*, 184-187.

Roberts, M. C. (1985). Book review of Stinson, R., & Stinson, P., *The long dying of baby Andrew.* *Journal of Pediatric Psychology, 10,* 110–112.

Roberts, M. C. (1986a). Failure to provide psychosocial services is institutional abuse. *Children's Health Care, 14,* 1–2.

Roberts, M. C. (1986b). The future of children's health care: What do we do? *Journal of Pediatric Psychology, 11,* 3–14.

Roberts, M. C. (1986c). Health promotion and problem prevention in pediatric psychology: An overview. *Journal of Pediatric Psychology, 11,* 147–161.

Roberts, M. C., Beidleman, W. B., & Wurtele, S. K. (1981). Children's perceptions of medical and psychological disorders in their peers. *Journal of Clinical Child Psychology, 10,* 76–78.

Roberts, M. C., & Broadbent, M. (1986). *Preschoolers and car passenger safety: Increasing usage with indigenous staff.* Manuscript submitted for publication.

Roberts, M. C., Elkins, P. D., & Royal, G. P. (1984). Psychological applications to the prevention of accidents and illness. In M. C. Roberts & L. Peterson (Eds.), *Prevention of problems in childhood: Psychological research and applications* (pp. 173–199). New York: Wiley-Interscience.

Roberts, M. C., Erickson, M. T., & Tuma, J. M. (1985). Addressing the needs: Guidelines for training psychologists to work with children, youth, and families. *Journal of Clinical Child Psychology, 14,* 70–79.

Roberts, M. C., & Fanurik, D. (1986). Rewarding elementary school children for their use of safety belts. *Health Psychology, 5,* 185–196.

Roberts, M. C., Fanurik, D., & Elkins, P. D. (in press). Training the child health psychologist. In P. Karoly & C. May (Eds.), *Handbook of child health assessment: Biopsychosocial perspectives.* New York: Wiley-Interscience.

Roberts, M. C., Fanurik, D., & Wilson, D. R. (1986). *A community program to reward children's use of seat belts.* Paper presented at the convention of the American Psychological Association, Washington, DC.

Roberts, M. C., & Horner, M. A. (1979). A comprehensive intervention for failure-to-thrive. *Journal of Clinical Child Psychology, 8,* 10–14.

Roberts, M. C., Johnson, A. Q., & Beidleman, W. B. (1984). The role of socioeconomic status in children's perceptions of medical and psychological disorders. *Journal of Clinical Child Psychology, 13,* 243–249.

Roberts, M. C., & La Greca, A. M. (1981). Behavioral assessment. In C. E. Walker (Ed.), *Clinical practice of psychology: A practical guide for mental health professionals* (pp. 293–346). New York: Pergamon.

Roberts, M. C., & Layfield, D. A. (in press). Promoting child passenger safety: A comparison of two positive methods. *Journal of Pediatric Psychology.*

Roberts, M. C., Lyman, R. D., Breiner, J., & Royal, G. P. (Eds.). (1982). *Publishing child-oriented articles in psychology: A compendium of publication outlets.* Washington, DC: University Press of America.

Roberts, M. C., & Maddux, J. E. (1982). A psychosocial conceptualization of nonorganic failure to thrive. *Journal of Clinical Child Psychology, 11,* 216–226.

Roberts, M. C., Maddux, J. E., & Wright, L. (1984). The developmental perspective in behavioral health. In J. D. Matarazzo, N. E. Miller, S. M. Weiss, J. A. Herd, & S. M. Weiss (Eds.), *Behavioral health: A handbook of health enhancement and disease prevention* (pp. 56–68). New York: Wiley-Interscience.

Roberts, M. C., Maddux, J., Wurtele, S. K., & Wright, L. (1982). Pediatric psychology: Health care clinical psychology for children. In T. Millon, C. J. Green, & R. B. Meagher (Eds.), *Handbook of clinical health psychology* (pp. 191–226). New York: Plenum.

Roberts, M. C., & Ottinger, D. R. (1979). A case study: Encopretic adolescent with multiple problems. *Journal of Clinical Child Psychology, 8,* 15–17.

Roberts, M. C., Ottinger, D. R., & Hannemann, R. E. (1977). *On treating childhood encopresis*. Unpublished manuscript, Purdue University.

Roberts, M. C., & Peterson, L. (1984a). Prevention models: Theoretical and practical implications. In M. C. Roberts & L. Peterson (Eds.), *Prevention of problems in childhood: Psychological research and applications* (pp. 1–39). New York: Wiley-Interscience.

Roberts, M. C., & Peterson, L. (Eds.). (1984b). *Prevention of problems in childhood: Psychological research and applications*. New York: Wiley-Interscience.

Roberts, M. C., Quevillon, R. P., & Wright, L. (1979). Pediatric psychology: A developmental report and survey of the literature. *Child and Youth Services, 2*(1), 1–9.

Roberts, M. C., & Turner, D. S. (1984). Preventing death and injury in childhood: A synthesis of child safety seat efforts. *Health Education Quarterly, 11*, 181–193.

Roberts, M. C., & Turner, D. S. (1986). Rewarding parents for their children's use of safety seats. *Journal of Pediatric Psychology, 11*, 25–36.

Roberts, M. C., & Wright, L. (1982). Role of the pediatric psychologist as consultant to pediatricians. In J. Tuma (Ed.), *Handbook for the practice of pediatric psychology* (pp. 251–289). New York: Wiley-Interscience.

Roberts, M. C., & Wurtele, S. K. (1980). On the noncompliant research subject in a study of medical noncompliance. *Social Science & Medicine, 14A*, 171.

Roberts, M. C., Wurtele, S. K., Boone, R. R., Ginther, L., & Elkins, P. (1981). Reduction of medical fears by use of modeling: A preventive application in a general population of children. *Journal of Pediatric Psychology, 6*, 293–300.

Robinson, E. A., & Eyberg, S. M. (1984). Behavioral assessment in pediatric settings: Theory, method, and application. In P. R. Magrab (Ed.), *Psychological and behavioral assessment: Impact on pediatric care* (pp. 91–140). New York: Plenum.

Rogers, D. E., Blendon, R. J., & Hearn, R. P. (1981). Some observations of pediatrics: Its past, present, and future. *Pediatrics, 67*, 776–884.

Routh, D. K., & Schroeder, C. S. (1976). Standardized playroom measures as indices of hyperactivity. *Journal of Abnormal Child Psychology, 4*, 199–207.

Routh, D. K., Schroeder, C. S., & O'Tuama, L. A. (1974). Development of activity level in children. *Developmental Psychology, 10*, 163–168.

Roy, R. (1982). *Where's buddy?* New York: Clarion.

Russo, D. C., Bird, B. L., & Masek, B. J. (1980). Assessment issues in behavioral medicine. *Behavioral Assessment, 2*, 1–18.

Rutter, M. (1979). Maternal deprivation, 1972–1978: New findings, new concepts, new approaches. *Child Development, 50*, 283–305.

Sachs, E. A. (1981). *Just like always*. New York: Antheneum.

Salk, L. (1969, September). The purposes and functions of the psychologist in a pediatric setting. In *Issues concerning the expansion of psychology within pediatric settings*. Symposium presented at the 77th Annual Convention of the American Psychological Association, Washington, DC.

Salk, L. (1978). *What every child would like his parents to know about divorce*. New York: Harper & Row.

Salk, L. (1985, August). *Looking back at my years in pediatric psychology*. Paper presented at the annual convention of the American Psychological Association, Los Angeles.

Sank, L. I., & Biglan, A. (1974). Operant treatment of a case of recurrent abdominal pain in a 10-year-old boy. *Behavior Therapy, 5*, 677–681.

Saslawsky, D. A., & Wurtele, S. K. (1986). Educating children about sexual abuse: Implications for pediatric intervention and possible prevention. *Journal of Pediatric Psychology, 11*, 235–245.

Schroeder, C. S. (1979). Psychologists in a private pediatric practice. *Journal of Pediatric Psychology, 4*, 5–18.

Schroeder, C. S., Goolsby, E., & Stangler, S. (1975). Preventive services in a private pediatric practice. *Journal of Clinical Child Psychology, 4,* 32–33.

Schroeder, C. S., Gordon, B. N., Kanoy, K., & Routh, D. K. (1983). Management of behavior problems in pediatric primary care settings. In M. Wolraich & D. K. Routh (Eds.), *Advances in developmental and behavioral pediatrics* (Vol. 4, pp. 25–86). Greenwich, CT: JAI.

Schroeder, C. S., Gordon, B. N., & McConnell, P. (1984a). Books for parents and children: Sexuality education. *Journal of Clinical Child Psychology, 13,* 203–208.

Schroeder, C. S., Gordon, B. N., & McConnell, P. (1984b). Books for parents and children: Divorce. *Journal of Clinical Child Psychology, 13,* 317–323.

Schroeder, C. S., Gordon, B. N., & McConnell, P. (1985). Books for parents and children on learning disabilities. *Journal of Clinical Child Psychology, 14,* 257–263.

Schwartz, G. E., & Weiss, S. M. (1978). Yale Conference on Behavioral Medicine: A proposed definition and statement of goals. *Journal of Behavioral Medicine, 1,* 3–12.

Shaw, W. J., & Walker, C. E. (1979). Use of relaxation in the short-term treatment of fetishistic behavior: An exploratory case study. *Journal of Pediatric Psychology, 4,* 403–407.

Sheffield, M. (1973). *Where do babies come from?* New York: Knopf.

Sibinga, M. S. (1983). The gastrointestinal tract. In M. D. Levine, W. B. Carey, A. C. Crocker, & R. T. Gross (Eds.), *Developmental-behavioral pediatrics* (pp. 482–487). Philadelphia: Saunders.

Siegel, L. (1983). Hospitalization and medical care of children. In C. E. Walker & M. C. Roberts (Eds.), *Handbook of clinical child psychology* (pp. 1089–1108). New York: Wiley-Interscience.

Simon, G., & Cohen, M. (1985). *The parent's pediatric companion.* New York: William Morrow.

Sinberg, J. (1979). *Divorce is a grown up problem: A book about divorce for young children and their parents.* New York: Avon.

Smith, S. D., Rosen, D., Trueworthy, R. C., & Lowman, J. T. (1979). A reliable method for evaluating drug compliance in children with cancer. *Cancer, 43,* 169–173.

Sobol, H. L. (1977). *My brother Steven is retarded.* New York: Macmillan.

Spinetta, J. J., Elliott, E. S., Hennessey, J. S., Knapp, V. S., Sheposh, J. P., Sparta, S. N., & Sprigle, R. P. (1982). The pediatric psychologist's role in catastrophic illness: Research and clinical issues. In J. M. Tuma (Ed.), *Handbook for the practice of pediatric psychology* (pp. 165–227). New York: Wiley-Interscience.

Spock, B., & Rothenberg, M. B. (1985). *Dr. Spock's baby and child care.* New York: Pocket Books.

St. Lawrence, J. S., & Drabman, R. S. (1983). Interruption of self-excoriation in a pediatric burn victim. *Journal of Pediatric Psychology, 8,* 155–159.

Stabler, B. (1979). Emerging models of psychologist–pediatrician liaison. *Journal of Pediatric Psychology, 4,* 307–313.

Stabler, B., Fernald, G. W., Johnson, M. R., Johnson, M. P., & Ryan, J. J. (1981). *Facilitating positive psychosocial adaptation in children with cystic fibrosis by increasing family communication and problem-solving skills.* Research report to the Cystic Fibrosis Foundation, University of North Carolina, Chapel Hill, NC.

Stanek, M. (1980). *Who's afraid of the dark?.* New York: Albert Whitman.

Stinson, R., & Stinson, P. (1983). *The long dying of Baby Andrew.* Boston: Little, Brown.

Sullivan, B. J. (1979a). Adjustment in diabetic adolescent girls: I. Development of the diabetic adjustment scale. *Psychosomatic Medicine, 41,* 119–126.

Sullivan, B. J. (1979b). Adjustment in diabetic adolescent girls: II. Adjustment, self-esteem, and depression in diabetic adolescent girls. *Psychosomatic Medicine, 41,* 127–138.

Tinsley, B. R., & Parke, R. D. (1984). The historical and contemporary relationship between developmental psychology and pediatrics: A review and an empirical survey. In H. E. Fitzgerald, B. M. Lester, & M. W. Yogman (Eds.), *Theory and research in behavioral pediatrics* (Vol. 2, pp. 1–30). New York: Plenum.

Treiber, F. A. (1986). A comparison of the positive and negative consequences approaches upon care restraint usage. *Journal of Pediatric Psychology, 11,* 15–24.

Van Vechten, D., Satterwhite, B., & Pless, I. B. (1977). Health education literature for parents of physically handicapped children. *American Journal of Diseases of Childhood, 131,* 311–315.

Varni, J. W. (1983). *Clinical behavioral pediatrics: An interdisciplinary biobehavioral approach.* New York: Pergamon.

Varni, J. W., & Dietrich, S. L. (1981). Behavioral pediatrics: Toward a reconceptualization. *Behavioral Medicine Update, 3,* 5–7.

Varni, J. W., Katz, E. R., & Dash, J. (1982). Behavioral and neurochemical aspects of pediatric pain. In T. J. Coates (Ed.), *Behavioral medicine: A practical handbook.* New York: Plenum.

Viorst, J. (1972). *The tenth good thing about Barney.* New York: Atheneum.

Walker, C. E. (1978). Toilet training, enuresis, and encopresis. In P. R. Magrab (Ed.), *Psychological management of pediatric problems: Vol. 1. Early life conditions and chronic diseases* (pp. 129–189). Baltimore: University Park Press.

Walker, C. E. (1979a). Behavioral intervention in a pediatric setting. In J. R. McNamara (Ed.), *Behavioral approaches to medicine: Application and analysis* (pp. 227–266). New York: Plenum.

Walker, C. E. (1979b). Behavioral therapy. In L. Wright, A. B. Schaefer, & G. Solomons (Eds.), *Encyclopedia of pediatric psychology* (pp. 83–103). Baltimore: University Park Press.

Walker, C. E., Bonner, B. L., & Kaufman, K. L. (in press). *The physically and sexually abused child: Evaluation and treatment.* New York: Pergamon.

Walker, C. E., Miller, M., & Smith, R. (1985). An introduction to pediatric psychology. In P. A. Keller & L. G. Ritt (Eds.), *Innovations in clinical practice: A source book* (Vol. 4, pp. 415–434). Sarasota, FL: Professional Resource Exchange.

Walker, L. J. S., & Healy, M. (1980). Psychological treatment of a burned child. *Journal of Pediatric Psychology, 5,* 395–404.

Wallerstein, J. S. (1983). Separation, divorce, and remarriage. In M. D. Levine, W. B. Carey, A. C. Crocker, & R. T. Gross (Eds.), *Developmental-behavioral pediatrics* (pp. 241–255). Philadelphia: Saunders.

Waye, M. F. (1979). Behavioral treatment of a child displaying comic-book mediated fear of hand shrinking: A case study. *Journal of Pediatric Psychology, 4,* 43–47.

Weaver, S. J. (Ed.). (1984). *Testing children.* Kansas City, MO: Test Corporation of America.

Webb, T. E., & Van Devere, C. A. (1985). *The structured pediatric psychosocial interview (SPPI) manual.* Akron, OH: Fourier.

Weiss, L., Katzman, M., & Wolchik, S. (1985). *Treating bulimia: A psychoeducational approach.* New York: Pergamon.

White, E. B. (1952). *Charlotte's web.* New York: Harper & Row.

Whitt, J. K., Dykstra, W., & Taylor, C. A. (1979). Children's conceptions of illness and cognitive development: Implications for pediatric practitioners. *Clinical Pediatrics, 18,* 327–339.

Williams, B. J., Foreyt, J. P., & Goodrick, G. K. (1981). *Pediatric behavioral medicine.* New York: Praeger.

Willis, D. J., Culbertson, J. L., & Mertens, R. A. (1984). Considerations in physical and health related disorders. In S. J. Weaver (Ed.), *Testing children* (pp.185–196). Kansas City, MO: Test Corporation of America.

Wisely, D. W., Masur, F. T., & Morgan, S. B. (1983). Psychological aspects of severe burn injuries in children. *Health Psychology, 2,* 45–72.

Wolchik, S. A., Braver, S. L., & Sandler, I. N. (1985). Maternal versus joint custody: Children's postseparation experiences and adjustment. *Journal of Clinical Child Psychology, 14,* 5–10.

Wolman, B. B. (1978). *Children's fears.* New York: Putnam.

Wolraich, M., & Routh, D. K. (Eds.). (1981–1983). *Advances in development and behavioral pediatrics* (Vols. 1–4). Greenwich, CT: JAI.

Wright, L. (1967). The pediatric psychologist: A role model. *American Psychologist, 22,* 323–325.

Wright, L. (1971). Conditioning of consummatory responses in young children. *Journal of Clinical*

Psychology, 27, 416–420.

Wright, L. (1973). Handling the encopretic child. *Professional Psychology, 4,* 137–144.

Wright, L. (1975). Outcome of a standardized program for treating psychogenic encopresis. *Professional Psychology, 6,* 453–456.

Wright, L. (1977). Conceptualizing and defining psychosomatic disorders. *American Psychologist, 32,* 625–628.

Wright, L. (1978a). Assessing the psychosomatic status of children. *Journal of Clinical Child Psychology, 7,* 94–112.

Wright, L. (1978b). Primary health care physicians to assume expanded role. *Feelings and their medical significance, 20,* 1–4.

Wright, L. (1979a). A comprehensive program for mental health and behavioral medicine in a large children's hospital. *Professional Psychology, 10,* 458–466.

Wright, L. (1979b). Health care psychology: Prospects for well-being of children. *American Psychologist, 34,* 1001–1006.

Wright, L. (1980). The standardization of compliance procedures, or the mass production of ugly ducklings. *American Psychologist, 35,* 119–122.

Wright, L. (1981). *Parent power: A guide to responsible childrearing.* New York: Bantam.

Wright, L. (1985). Psychology and pediatrics: Prospects for cooperative efforts to promote child health: A discussion with Morris Green. *American Psychologist, 40,* 949–952.

Wright, L., & Jimmerson, S. (1971). Intellectual sequelae of hemophilus influenzae meningitis. *Journal of Abnormal Psychology, 77,* 181–183.

Wright, L., Nunnery, A., Eichel, B. & Scott, R. (1968). Application of conditioning principles to problems of tracheostomy addiction in children. *Journal of Consulting and Clinical Psychology, 32,* 603–606.

Wright, L., Nunnery, A., Eichel, B., & Scott, R. (1969). Behavioral tactics for reinstating natural breathing in tracheostomy-addicted infants. *Pediatric Research, 3,* 275–278.

Wright, L., Schaefer, A. B., & Solomons, G. (1979). *Encyclopedia of pediatric psychology.* Baltimore: University Park Press.

Wright, L., & Thalassinos, P. A. (1973). Success with electroshock in habitual vomiting. *Clinical Pediatrics, 12,* 594–597.

Wright, L., & Walker, C. E. (1977). Treating the encopretic child. *Clinical Pediatrics, 16,* 1042–1045.

Wright, L., Woodcock, J. M., & Scott, R. (1970). Treatment of sleep disturbance in a young child by conditioning. *Southern Medical Journal, 44,* 969–972.

Wyman, P. A., Cowen, E. L., Hightower, A. D., & Pedro-Carroll, J. L. (1985). Perceived competence, self-esteem, and anxiety in latency-aged children of divorce. *Journal of Clinical Child Psychology, 14,* 20–26.

Yeaton, W. H., & Bailey, J. S. (1978). Teaching pedestrian safety skills to young children: An analysis and one-year followup. *Journal of Applied Behavior Analysis, 11,* 315–329.

Yokley, J. M., & Glenwick, D. S. (1984). Increasing the immunization of preschool children: An evaluation of applied community interventions. *Journal of Applied Behavior Analysis, 17,* 313–325.

Author Index

Abikoff, H., 58
Adams, B., 41
Adams, D. W., 41
Achenbach, T. M., 18, 37
Allen, C. M., 36
Als, H., 56
American Medical Association, 51
American Psychiatric Association, 69, 76
Anderson, F. P., 2
Anderson, G. S., 41
Anderson, H. W., 41
Aradine, C. R., 40
Arasteh, J. D., 90
Arthur, J. L., 92
Asken, M. J., 5
Association for the Care of Children's
    Health, 84
Athreya, B. H., 51
Atkeson, B. M., 37
Axelrod, S., 91
Azrin, N. H., 12, 15, 30, 37, 38, 41, 43

Baer, R. A., 64
Bailey, J. S., 84
Baker, L., 73
Baker, S. P., 92
Barkley, R. A., 37, 93
Barnard, J. D., 30, 81
Barness, L. A., 91
Barnett, H. L., 91
Barr, G., 36

Barrios, B. A., 37
Bayley, N., 55
Beales, J. G., 94
Becker, J. V., 63, 72
Becker, W. C., 40
Beidleman, W. B., 66
Bell, L. S., 9, 10, 51
Benjamin, P., 24, 45, 47, 51, 52
Berger, M. E., 3
Bergey, S. F. A., 70
Bergman, A. B., 9, 42
Berman, R. E., 91
Bernstein, J. E., 41
Bernstein, N. R., 10
Besalel, V. A., 30, 41
Bessman, C. A., 58
Bibace, R., 66
Biglan, A., 72
Bird, B. L., 59
Blendon, R. J., 9
Blount, R. L., 64
Blum, R. W., 92
Blume, J., 41
Boat, T. F., 58, 65
Bonner, B. L., 80
Bonsall, C., 41
Boone, R. R., 83
Boyer, W., 65
Braver, S. L., 80
Brazelton, T. B., 56, 81
Breiner, J., 89

Brewer, D., 48
Brion-Meisels, L. A., 30
Broadbent, M., 85
Bronheim, S. M., 64
Brooks, R. B., 41
Brouwer, R., 84
Brown, M. W., 41
Browne, A., 95
Brownlee-Duffeck, M., 44, 82, 93
Brunette, R., 70
Burgess, D., 36, 56
Burnett, R. D., 9, 10, 51
Burns, B. J., 24, 25, 29, 32, 34
Burns, W. J., 70, 72, 73, 90
Butler, J. F., 43
Caldwell, S., 58
Cameron, J. R., 81
Campbell, S. B., 18
Card, A. L., 46
Carey, W. B., 6, 91
Cataldo, M. F., 58, 62, 90
Cautela, J., 30
Chapman, J., 70
Chenkin, C. G., 46
Christian, W. P., 73, 91
Christophersen, E. R., 30, 81, 38–40, 79, 81, 85, 93
Chwast, R., 24, 45, 48, 51, 52
Cilotta, C., 41
Cleland, C. I., 76, 94
Coates, T., 95
Cohen, M., 40
Conners, C. K., 37
Cowen, E. L., 79
Cox, M., 79
Cox, R., 79
Crawford, P., 64, 65, 81
Creer, T. L., 68, 73, 91
Crocker, A. C., 6, 91
Cromer, W. W., 24, 25, 29, 32, 34
Culbertson, J. L., 64
Cullen, P. M., 46
Cunningham, C. E., 63
Cunningham, S. J., 30, 70
Curry, F., 63
Cuvo, A. J., 72
Cytryn, L., 57

Dahlquist, L. M., 64
Dash, J., 69
Dassel, S. W., 9
D'Astous, J., 70
Davis, P. K., 72
Dawson, G., 76
Deasy-Spinetta, P., 92
Dershewitz, R. A., 81
Deveau, E. J., 41
Dietrich, S. L., 6
Division of Health Psychology, 5
DiVitto, B. A., 94
Doershuk, C. F., 58, 65
Drabman, R. S., 30, 60, 68, 78, 79
Drotar, D., 21, 24, 25, 29, 45, 48, 51, 52, 58, 64, 65, 81
Duff, R. S., 2, 3
Dunbar, J. M., 94
Dunn, J., 70
Dunn-Geier, J., 70
Dykstra, W., 66, 83

Edelmann, C. M., Jr., 91
Eichel, B., 17, 49
Elkins, P. D., 19, 22, 44, 80–84, 92, 93
Elliott, C. H., 17, 58
Elliott, E. S., 15
Engel, G. L., 50
Epstein, L. H., 84
Erickson, M. T., 19
Eudy, C., 68
Eyberg, S. M., 57, 78

Falliers, C. J., 73, 91
Fandal, A. W., 36, 56
Fanurik, D., 19, 22, 85
Farber, S. S., 95
Farmer, L., 84
Fassler, J., 41
Feldman, G., 73
Feldman, W., 90
Felner, R. D., 95
Fernald, G. W., 65
Ferrari, M., 18
Finch, A. J., 92
Finkelhor, D., 95

Firestone, P., 90
Fischer, S. G., 30
Fitch, P., 57
Fitzgerald, H. E., 90
Fleischman, M. J., 92
Fordyce, W. E., 71
Forehand, R., 30, 37, 58, 78, 92
Foreyt, J. P., 6
Forgatch, M. S., 78
Foxx, R. M., 13, 15, 30, 37, 38, 41, 43
Frankenburg, W. K., 36, 56
Fras, J., 10
Friedman, R. M., 37
Funk, M. J., 30, 64

Gaiter, J. L., 94
Ganofsky, M. A., 64, 65, 81
Gardner, R. A., 41
Geist, R. A., 48
Ginther, L., 83
Gittleman-Klein, K., 58
Glennon, B., 58
Glenwick, D. S., 34
Goldberg, A. W., 94
Goodman, J. T., 70
Goodrick, G. K., 6
Goolsby, E., 46
Gordon, B. N., 40, 46
Gordon, J., 41
Gordon, S., 41
Gottfried, A. W., 56, 94
Gottlieb, M. I., 59
Green, C., 90
Green, M., 6, 70
Gross, A. M., 68
Gross, R. T., 6, 91
Grossman, C. S., 40
Gruenberg, S. M., 41
Guerin, D., 56
Gullion, M. E., 40
Gullo, S. V., 41
Gyulay, J. E., 30, 85

Handleman, J. S., 93
Haney, J. I., 84
Hannemann, R. E., 1, 31, 51, 62
Harper, R. B., 78

Harries, J., 41
Harris, S. L., 18, 93
Hartlage, L. C., 11
Hartlage, P. L., 11
Hartmann, D. P., 37
Hayes, M. L., 41
Hazen, B. S., 41
Healy, M., 2, 17, 60
Hearn, R. P., 9
Hennessey, J. S., 15
Herd, J. A., 90, 95
Hermes, P., 41
Hernandez, M., 37
Hetherington, E. M., 79
Hightower, A. D., 79
Hilgard, J., 1, 17, 44
Hillman, H. S., 84
Hirsch, D. L. O., 73
Hobbs, N., 92
Hodges, K., 57
Hoffman, J. I. E., 91
Holmes, D. L., 94
Horne, A. M., 92
Horner, M. A., 1, 33, 51, 58, 63, 75, 76
Howe, J., 41
Humphreys, P., 30, 70

Ialongo, N. S., 46
Ingersoll, B., 63
Ireton, H., 55, 56

Jacobstein, D. M., 64
Jarvie, G., 30, 60, 79
Jason, L. A., 95
Jay, S. M., 58
Jeans, M. E., 94
Jewitt, C. L., 93
Jimmerson, S., 59
Johnson, A. Q., 66
Johnson, G., 70
Johnson, M. P., 65
Johnson, M. R., 65
Jones, C. R., 41
Jones, J. G., 30, 94
Jones, R. T., 84

Kagan, J., 2

Kanoy, K. W., 19–21, 46, 51, 78
Karoly, P., 6, 54, 90, 91
Katz, E. R., 69
Katz, K. S., 37
Katzman, M., 73, 91
Kaufman, K. L., 80
Kaye, R., 91
Kazdin, A. E., 84, 90
Keene, D., 70
Keene, W. M., 47
Kellerman, J., 92
Kelley, M. L., 60
Kelly, J. A., 95
Kenny, T. J., 70
Kerasotes, D., 94
Klein, D. J., 58
Kline, J., 57
Klinzing, D. G., 83
Klinzing, D. R., 83
Knapp, V. S., 15
Knitzer, J., 3
Knudson-Cooper, M. S., 92
Koeppen, A. S., 16
Kolko, D. J., 14
Koocher, G. P., 15, 47, 92
Krasnegor, N. A., 90
Kratochwill, T. R., 1, 13, 51, 72, 91
Krementz, J., 41
Kucia, C., 58

La Greca, A. M., 6, 33, 54, 57, 58, 68
Lahey, B. B., 90, 94
Latter, J., 70
Lavigne, J. V., 70, 72, 73, 90
Layfield, D. A., 85
LeBaron, S., 1, 17, 44
LeBow, M. D., 94
LeClaire, S., 85
Leon, G. R., 94
Lester, B. M., 56, 90
Levine, E. S., 41
Levine, M. D., 6, 91
Levy, R. L., 84
Lewis, M., 93
Lewis, S., 40, 48
Lichtenstein, R., 55
Liebman, R., 73

Linscheid, T. R., 62, 63
Litt, C., 24, 45, 48, 51, 52
Livingston, C., 41
Lodish, D., 84
Lowe, K., 1, 27, 45, 67
Lowman, J. T., 67
Lutzker, J. R., 1, 27, 45, 67
Lyman, R. D., 69, 74, 79, 89
Lynch, M., 41

MacPhee, D., 39
Madden, N. A., 58, 62
Maddux, J. E., 6, 12, 18, 19, 48, 54, 74, 75, 81
Magid, K., 41
Magrab, P. R., 54, 56, 67, 90, 91
Masek, B. J., 59
Mash, E. J., 54, 57, 58, 91
Masur, F. T., 7, 59, 92
Matarazzo, J. D., 6, 85, 90, 95
Matarazzo, R. G., 78
Matson, J. L., 43
Matthews, L., 58, 65
May, C., 54, 91
McClelland, C. Q., 3
McCollum, A. T., 92
McConnell, P., 40
McGrath, P. J., 30, 70, 71, 90
McKay, R. J., 36, 37, 50, 81
McKnew, D., 57
McMahon, R. J., 30, 58, 78, 92
McNeer, M. F., 60
Meagher, R., 90
Melamed, B. G., 82
Mertens, R. A., 64
Mesibov, G. B., 19, 21, 46, 76
Metz, J. R., 36
Meyer, C., 56
Mezey, A. P., 91
Middlebrook, J. L., 60
Miller, A. J., 1, 13, 51, 72
Miller, M., 19, 24
Miller, N. E., 90, 95
Millon, T., 90
Minuchin, S., 73
Morgan, J. R., 46
Morgan, S. B., 59, 77, 92

Morgan, W. L., 50
Mori, L., 84
Moritsugu, J. N., 95
Morris, R. J., 91
Mullins, L. L., 30, 64
Munford, P. R., 72
Murray, J. A., 84

National Center for Health Statistics, 37
Neeper, R., 94
Nelson, W. E., 36, 37, 50, 81
Newcomb, A. F., 46
Nunnery, A., 17, 49

O'Dougherty, M. M., 93
O'Grady, D. J., 6, 90
Ollendick, T. H., 43
Olmsted, R. W., 9
Olson, R. A., 17, 30, 64
Oski, F. A., 91
Osman, B. B., 41
Ottinger, D. R., 1, 17, 19-21, 27, 31, 33, 47, 51, 62, 68
O'Tuama, L. A., 58
Ozolins, M., 58

Pally, R., 72
Papadopoulou, Z., 67
Parke, R. D., 18
Parker, L. H., 58
Pasternak, J. F., 94
Patterson, G. R., 40, 78, 92
Pawlack-Floyd, C., 84
Pearson, J. E. R., 58
Pedro-Carroll, J. L., 79
Perlman, J. L., 66
Perrin, J. M., 92
Perry, C., 95
Peterson, A., 95
Peterson, L., 34, 42, 44, 80, 82, 84, 93, 95
Phillips, D., 30
Pless, I. B., 40
Poche, C., 84
Potter, P. C., 66, 67
Powers, M. D., 93
Prugh, D. G., 73, 74, 91

Quevillon, R. P., 48

Rainey, S. K., 30, 31, 79, 81
Rando, T. A., 93
Rapoff, K. E., 79
Rapoff, M. A., 30, 31, 38, 39, 79, 93
Reich, J. N., 94
Renne, C. M., 68, 73, 91
Rheingold, H. L., 77
Rice, D. C., 81
Richardson, G. M., 30
Rickard-Figueroa, J. L., 14
Robertson, L. S., 92
Roberts, M. D., 1, 3, 6, 12, 17-22, 24, 27, 31, 33-35, 44, 47, 48, 51, 54, 57, 58, 62, 63, 66, 67, 69, 74-76, 79-85, 89, 90, 92, 93, 95
Robinson, E. A., 57
Rogers, D. E., 9
Rogers, M. C., 58
Rosen, D., 67
Rosenbaum, M. S., 30, 78
Ross, D. M., 93
Ross, S. A., 93
Rothenberg, M. B., 40, 81
Routh, D. K., 46, 58, 66, 90
Rowe, D. S., 2
Roy, R., 41
Royal, G. P., 19, 81, 84, 89, 92
Rudolph, A. M., 91
Russo, D. C., 58, 59, 62, 73, 90
Rutter, M., 75
Ryan, J. J., 65

Sachs, E. A., 41
Sajwaj, T. E., 63, 72
Salk, L., 12, 24, 41, 80
Sallan, S. E., 15
Sandler, S., 37, 80
Sanger, S., 10
Sank, L. I., 72
Saslawsky, D. A., 80
Satterwhite, B., 40
Saylor, C. F., 92
Schaefer, A. B., 7, 55, 56, 59, 64, 69, 70, 73, 74, 90

Schaefer, C. E., 93
Schillinger, J., 70
Schreibman, W., 41
Schroeder, C. S., 19–21, 40, 46, 51, 58, 78
Schwartz, G. E., 5
Sciarillo, W., 36, 56
Scissors, C., 84
Scott, R., 17, 30, 49
Seligman, M., 93
Shaw, W. J., 17
Sheffield, M., 41
Shelov, S. P., 91
Sheposh, J. P., 15
Shigetomi, C., 37
Shinefield, H. R., 36
Sibinga, M. S., 72
Siegel, L. J., 44, 82, 93
Simon, G., 40
Sinberg, J., 41
Singh, R., 30
Sledden, E. A., 19
Smith, R., 19, 24
Smith, S. D., 67
Sneed, T. J., 30
Sobol, H. L., 41
Solomons, G., 7, 55, 56, 59, 64, 69, 70, 73, 74, 90
Sosland-Edelman, D., 85
Sourkes, B. M., 47
Sparta, S. N., 15
Spencer, J. E., 56
Spinetta, J. J., 15, 92
Spock, B., 40, 81
Sprigle, R. P., 15
Stabler, B., 13, 24, 25, 29, 32, 65, 72
Stanek, M., 41
Stangler, S., 46
Staples, W. P., 3
Steffen, J. J., 6, 90
Stern, L., 57, 58
Stern, R. C., 65
Stinson, P., 34, 35
Stinson, R., 34, 35
St. Lawrence, J. S., 60
Stone, W. L., 6
Stunkard, A. J., 94

Sullivan, B. J., 65
Swearingen, M., 84

Taft, L. T., 93
Taylor, C. A., 66, 83
Terdel, L. G., 55, 57, 58, 91
Thalassinos, P. A., 63
Thwing, E., 56
Tinsley, B. R., 18
Toobert, D. J., 78
Treiber, F. A., 85
Tronick, E. Z., 56
Trueworthy, R. C., 67
Tuma, J. M., 19, 90
Turner, D. S., 85
Turner, S. M., 63, 72

Vajner, P., 24, 25, 45, 48, 51, 52
Van Devere, C. A., 56
Van Vechten, D., 40
Varni, J. W., 6, 30, 69, 90, 94
Vaughan, V. C., 36, 37, 50, 81, 91
Viorst, J., 41

Walker, C. E., 3, 4, 10, 12, 17–21, 24, 25, 30, 33, 38, 48, 51, 60, 62, 69, 80, 90, 93, 94
Walker, L. J. S., 2, 17, 60
Wallander, J. L., 94
Wallerstein, J. S., 79, 80
Walsh, N. E., 66
Waye, M. F., 17
Weaver, S. J., 55, 91
Webb, T. E., 56
Wedgewood, R. J., 9
Weisberg, I., 3
Weiss, L., 73, 91
Weiss, S. M., 5, 90, 95
Weisz, J. R., 58
Wesson, L., 19, 21, 46
White, E. B., 41
Whitt, J. K., 66, 83
Williams, B. J., 6
Williams, M. K., 9
Willis, D. J., 64
Wilson, D. R., 85
Wisely, D. W., 59, 92

Wolchik, S. A., 73, 80, 91
Wolf, M. M., 30
Wolfe, D. A., 37, 95
Wolman, B. B., 41
Wolraich, M., 90
Woodcock, J. M., 30
Wright, L., 2, 3, 6, 7, 10, 12, 14, 17–19, 24, 26, 30, 37–40, 48, 49, 51, 54–56, 59, 61–64, 68–70, 73, 74, 81, 90, 93

Wuori, D., 64
Wurtele, S. K., 12, 48, 66, 67, 80, 83
Wyman, P. A., 79

Yeaton, W. H., 84
Yogman, M. W., 90
Yokley, J. M., 34
Young-Hyman, D., 70

Subject Index

Abbreviations, medical, 49, 50
Abdominal pain, 1, 4, 13, 36, 51, 54, 69, 70–72
Abuse, 21, 34, 36, 37, 80, 95
 See also Sexual abuse
Acceptance by peers of disordered children, 66, 67
Adaptive Behavior Rating Scale, 37
Adjustment, 4, 21, 64–66, 69, 71, 77, 79, 80
Algorithms, 36, 37
American Academy of Pediatrics, 51, 86
Annals of Behavioral Medicine, 88
Anorexia nervosa, 33, 38, 54, 63, 72, 91
Anticipatory guidance, 10, 81, 82
Anxiety, 1, 4, 16, 17, 27, 31, 41, 43, 44, 58, 60, 68, 73, 91
 See also Fears
Assessment, 25, 37, 54–59, 91
Association for the Care of Children's Health, 83, 87
Asthma, 6, 38, 53, 67, 68, 73, 78, 91
Autism, 74, 76, 77

Bayley Scales of Infant Development, 36, 55, 74, 76
Behavior management and interventions, 9, 10, 11, 13, 16, 21, 30, 37, 40, 57
Behavioral health, 5, 6, 85, 90, 95
Behavioral medicine, 5
Behavioral Medicine Abstracts, 88

Behavioral pediatrics, 5, 6, 90
Bibliotherapy, 39–43, 60, 82
Blaming, 70, 71, 77
Bone marrow aspiration, 1, 4, 17, 44, 53
Books, *See* Bibliotherapy
Bowel movements, 15, 16, 17, 27, 61, 62
Buckle Up Bama's Future, 85
Bulimia, 72, 91
Burns, 1, 4, 17, 21, 34, 55, 59, 84, 92

Call in/Come in service, 19, 46, 78, 82
Cancer, 41, 64, 67, 92
Case conceptualization, 7, 14, 24, 49–51, 54, 70, 76
Case problems, 19, 20–22
Cerebral palsy, 33, 68
Child Assessment Schedule, 57
Child Health Alert, 89
Child health psychology, 6, 54, 90
Children's Defense Fund, 3
Children's Health Care, 87, 88
Chronic illness, 33, 48, 64, 65, 69, 84, 92
 See also Physical disorders, chronic
Clinical behavioral pediatrics, 6
Clinical Pediatrics, 40, 89
Crisis intervention, 47
Colitis, 73
Collaboration, 3, 23, 32
 See also Consultation
Collaborative team model, 32–35
Communication, 47, 49, 76

Compliance, *See* Noncompliance

Consultation, 2, 3, 7, 10, 11, 23, 24, 28,
    45–47, 51, 52, 64
  collaborative team, 32–35
  independent functions, 25–28, 78
  indirect, 28–32, 78
  models of, 25–52
  pediatric practice oriented, 35–52
  problems in, 31, 32, 48, 69

Contracting, 60, 62
Coping, 65, 71
Cystic fibrosis, 53, 58, 64, 65, 81

Death, 21, 41, 70, 83
Definitions, 5–7, 22
Denver Developmental Screening Test,
    36, 56
Development, normal, 3, 39, 46, 65, 66
Developmental assessment, 7, 18, 33, 36,
    53, 55, 56, 74, 76
Developmental–behavioral pediatrics, 6,
    10, 39, 46, 90, 91
Developmental disorders, 8, 20, 33, 46,
    74–77, 93
Developmental perspective, 7, 18, 54, 81
Diabetes, 1, 4, 6, 10, 27, 33, 44, 45, 52,
    53, 64–67, 78, 82
*Diagnostics and Statistical Manual of
    Mental Disorders*, 57, 60, 76
Diagnostic testing, 49, 54
Dialysis, 34, 67
Differential diagnosis, 49, 51, 61, 76
Division of Health Psychology, 5, 88
Divorce, 20, 28, 40, 41, 70, 79, 80

Eating disorders, *See* Feeding Disorders
Encopresis, 1, 4, 12, 15–18, 26–28, 30,
    31, 38, 51, 60–62, 68, 69, 93
Enuresis, 12, 31, 52, 68, 69, 93
Epilepsy, 44, 67
Ethan Has An Operation, 82

Failure to thrive, 1, 4, 12, 18, 33, 36, 51,
    53, 55, 56, 58, 62, 63, 74–76
Family, 20, 65, 66, 79
Family therapy, 66, 73
Fears

  general, 2, 16, 17, 20, 30, 37, 41, 61,
    91, 92
  medical, 18, 40, 43, 61, 80, 82
Feeding disorders, 14, 18, 20, 30, 33, 38,
    60, 62–64, 76, 94

Gesell Developmental Schedules, 37
Growth curves, 37

Handicaps, 33, 40, 53, 64, 68, 93
Health promotion, 3, 95
  See also Prevention
Health psychology, 5
Health Psychology, 88
Heart disease, 64, 66
Hemophilia, 4, 64
Hirschsprung's disease, 15, 16, 51, 60
Hospitalization, 4, 41, 42, 80, 82, 93
Hyperactivity, 18, 37, 58, 74, 78, 82, 93,
    94
Hypnosis, 44, 71

Immunization, 9, 34, 80
Independent functions consultation
    model, 25–28, 33, 78
Indirect consultation model, 28–32, 33, 78
Injuries, 21, 36, 59, 69, 80, 86, 92
Intellectual assessment, 18
Interviewing, 56–58
Inpatient medical settings, 9–11, 21, 24,
    48, 51, 81

Jargon, 23, 25, 49, 50, 77
Journal of Behavioral Medicine, 89
Journal of Clinical Child Psychology, 40, 89
*Journal of Developmental and Behavioral
    Pediatrics*, 88, 89
Journal of Pediatric Psychology, 87, 88

Latch-key children, 84
Lead poisoning, 37, 58, 61, 86
Learning disabilities, 9, 28, 37, 40, 41, 94
Let's Pretend Hospital, 83
Leukemia, 1, 6, 53, 78

Meningitis, 4, 59
Mental retardation, 41, 62, 74, 94

Metaphors, 67
Mind set, 12–15
Minnesota Child Development Inventory,
   56
Neonatal Behavioral Assessment Scale,
   56
Noncompliance
   behavioral, 14, 15, 28, 30, 38, 58, 78,
      79
   medical, 1, 6, 10, 21, 27, 28, 33, 38,
      44, 45, 52, 55, 65, 67–69, 73, 92,
      94
Nutrition, 4, 9, 34, 65

Obesity, 38, 94
Observations, 58, 59, 63, 70, 71
Oncology, 14, 21, 34, 47, 53
Otitis media, 59
Outpatient medical settings, 9, 11, 21,
   24, 25, 51, 81

Pain, 1, 13, 16, 17, 21, 30, 31, 42, 59, 68,
   69, 74, 94
Parenting Stress Index, 37
Parenting training, 43, 46, 65, 76, 78, 92
Paul and Dot Have a Hospital Experience,
   83
Pediatric Multiphasic Examination, 36
Pediatrics, 89
Pediatricians, 2, 10, 11, 18, 19, 23,
   27–29, 51
   settings, 4, 9, 11, 22, 24, 51, 54, 81
   time, 3, 9, 11, 32, 35, 39
Personality Inventory for Children, 37
Physical disorders, 20, 21, 84–86
   See also Somatic complaints and
      chronic illness
   acute, 7, 59, 64
   chronic, 7, 9, 21, 41, 64–68
Pica, 62
Pill swallowing, 30
Play therapy, 16, 60
Pragmatism, 17, 18, 22
Premack Principle, 14
Prematurity, 34, 53, 94
Preparation for medical events, 20, 34,
   42–44, 80, 82–84, 93

Prevention, 3, 5, 6, 8, 9, 34, 42, 54,
   81–86, 92, 93, 95
Problem-Oriented Medical Record, 50
Protocols, 29–31, 37–39, 85
Psychological–behavioral problems,
   77–80, 82–84
Psychopathology, 27, 77–80, 82–84
Psychosomatic disorders, 7, 68–74
Psychotherapy, 14, 76

Referrals, 4, 19–21, 25, 29, 37, 47, 48,
   52, 67
Reinforcement, 13, 30, 45, 61–63, 67, 71
Relaxation, 16, 27, 33, 60, 67, 71
Reports, 12, 25, 26, 50
Resources, 8, 87–95
Roles and functions of pediatric
   psychologists, 5, 7, 28
Ruling-out process, 51, 74
Rumination, 63, 72

Safe At Home, 84
Safety, 30, 54, 81, 84–86
School attendance and performance, 3, 9,
   13, 19, 21, 38, 70, 71
Screening, 34, 36, 37, 38
Seat belts, 4, 30, 54, 84–86
Sex education, 40, 41
Sexual abuse, 42, 54, 80, 95
Sleeping problems, 20, 29, 30
Structured interviewing, 56–58
Structured Pediatric Psychosocial
   Interview, 56, 57
SOAP notes, 50
Social skills, 27, 82
Society for Behavioral Pediatrics, 88
Society of Behavioral Medicine, 88
Society of Pediatric Psychology, 87, 88
Somatic complaints, 14, 20
Spina bifida, 4

Temper tantrums, 29, 30, 79
Terminal illness, 40, 55, 79
The Injury Prevention Program, 86
Theoretical orientations, 12, 17
Time-out, 13, 78, 79
Toilet training, 13, 15, 20, 30, 37, 38, 41,

43, 53, 93
Toothbrushing, 84
Tracheotomy addiction, 17, 18, 28, 49,
    53, 68
Turf issues, 23, 26, 32, 47–49

Ulcers, 74
Urination, 16

Vomiting, 63, 68, 72

Well child, 3, 9, 10, 11, 83

About the Author

Michael C. Roberts, PhD, is a professor in the Department of Psychology, The University of Alabama, and coordinator of the clinical child psychology concentration within its Clinical Training Program. He is a graduate of Purdue University and completed an internship in pediatric/clinical child psychology at Oklahoma Children's Memorial Hospital (Oklahoma University Health Sciences Center). Dr. Roberts has published numerous articles and chapters on social learning and pediatric/clinical child psychology topics. He has co-edited three books, including *Handbook of Clinical Child Psychology* (with C. Eugene Walker, 1983) and *Prevention of Problems in Childhood: Psychological Research and Applications* (with Lizette Peterson, 1984). He serves as associate editor of the *Journal of Pediatric Psychology* and is on the editorial boards of several journals. Dr. Roberts recently completed terms as president of the Society of Pediatric Psychology and on the board of directors of the Association for the Care of Children's Health. He conducts research, practice, and community programs in various aspects of children's health.

Psychology Practitioner Guidebooks

Editors
Arnold P. Goldstein, Syracuse University
Leonard Krasner, SUNY at Stony Brook
Sol L. Garfield, Washington University

Elsie M. Pinkston & Nathan L. Linsk—CARE OF THE ELDERLY: A Family Approach
Donald Meichenbaum—STRESS INOCULATION TRAINING
Sebastiano Santostefano—COGNITIVE CONTROL THERAPY WITH CHILDREN AND ADOLESCENTS
Lillie Weiss, Melanie Katzman & Sharlene Wolchik—TREATING BULIMIA: A Psychoeducational Approach
Edward B. Blanchard & Frank Andrasik—MANAGEMENT OF CHRONIC HEADACHES: A Psychological Approach
Raymond G. Romanczyk—CLINICAL UTILIZATION OF MICROCOMPUTER TECHNOLOGY
Philip H. Bornstein & Marcy T. Bornstein—MARITAL THERAPY: A Behavioral-Communications Approach
Michael T. Nietzel & Ronald C. Dillehay—PSYCHOLOGICAL CONSULTATION IN THE COURTROOM
Elizabeth B. Yost, Larry E. Beutler, M. Anne Corbishley & James R. Allender—GROUP COGNITIVE THERAPY: A Treatment Approach for Depressed Older Adults
Lillie Weiss—DREAM ANALYSIS IN PSYCHOTHERAPY
Edward A. Kirby & Liam K. Grimley—UNDERSTANDING AND TREATING ATTENTION DEFICIT DISORDER
Jon Eisenson—LANGUAGE AND SPEECH DISORDERS IN CHILDREN
Eva L. Feindler & Randolph B. Ecton—ADOLESCENT ANGER CONTROL: Cognitive-Behavioral Techniques
Michael C. Roberts—PEDIATRIC PSYCHOLOGY: Psychological Interventions and Strategies for Pediatric Problems
Daniel S. Kirschenbaum, William G. Johnson & Peter M. Stalonas, Jr.— TREATING CHILDHOOD AND ADOLESCENT OBESITY
W. Stewart Agras—EATING DISORDERS: Management of Obesity, Bulimia and Anorexia Nervosa